The Busy Grandma's Guide to

Guide to

Prayer

A GUIDED PRAYER JOURNAL

THE Motherhood CLUB

The Busy Grandma's Guide to

prayer

A GUIDED PRAYER JOURNAL

Lisa Whelchel & Gentry Coleman

HOWARD BOOKS
A DIVISION OF SIMON & SCHUSTER
New York   London   Toronto   Sydney

Lisa Whelchel is best known for her role as "Blair" on the long-running television comedy *The Facts of Life*. Now a homeschooling mother, speaker, and pastor's wife, she is the best-selling author of *Creative Correction, The Facts of Life and Other Lessons My Father Taught Me,* and *Taking Care of the Me in Mommy.* Lisa and her husband, Steve, are the cofounders of MomTime Ministries. They live in Texas with their children, Tucker, Haven, and Clancy.

www.LisaWhelchel.com

Gentry Coleman, Lisa's mother, is a multimillion-dollar commerical real estate broker, but her greatest success was raising her three children. Mrs. Coleman and her husband, Roy, divide their time between Los Angeles and Dallas.

Lisa's Dedication

It is an honor to dedicate this book to
my children's grandfather,

Roy Coleman

You have . . .
been center stage in all of their best memories,
satisfied the healthy need for the rough and tumble,
played a vital role in their emotional development, and
listened, fixed, cranked, taught, and played
with infinite patience. I am grateful for your
day-in, day-out influence as an authentic man of God.

Grandchildren are the crown of the aged.
Proverbs 17:6

Gentry's Dedication

What joy it brings me to dedicate this book
to my nine phenomenal grandchildren,

*Chasin, Jake, Tucker, Megan, Haven,
Clancy, Moriah, Serena, and Delaney.*

You make my life count!
I really think grandchildren are like Roth IRAs—
you pay up front, but when you're ready
to cash in, they're tax-free fun.

Our purpose at Howard Books is to:

- *Increase faith* in the hearts of growing Christians
- *Inspire holiness* in the lives of believers
- *Instill hope* in the hearts of struggling people everywhere

Because He's coming again!

HOWARD
BOOKS

Published by Howard Books, a division of Simon & Schuster
1230 Avenue of the Americas, New York, NY 10020
www.howardpublishing.com

The Busy Grandma's Guide to Prayer © 2006 by Lisa Whelchel and
Gentry Coleman

10 Digit ISBN: 1-58229-581-6; 13 Digit ISBN: 978-1-58229-581-7
10 Digit ISBN: 1-4165-3589-6; 13 Digit ISBN: 978-1-4165-3589-8

10 9 8 7 6 5 4 3 2 1

For information regarding special discounts for bulk purchases, please contact Simon &
Schuster Special Sales at 1-800-456-6798 or business@simonandschuster.com.

Edited by Between the Lines
Cover design by Diane Whisner and Cindy Sartain
Interior design by John Mark Luke Designs
Illustrations by Cindy Sartain

Contents

Contents

Day 5

Day 6

Day 7

Day 8

Day 9

Day 10

Day 11

Day 12

Contents

Day 13

Day 14

Day 15

Day 16

Contents

Day 17

Day 18

Day 19

Day 20

Lisa's Introduction

I received the following e-mail from my mother, Gentry Coleman, just this morning. I'd better give you a bit of back story before you read it, or you'll be completely lost.

Casey, my mother's youngest son, is getting married soon, so Mom is in the throes of planning a bridal shower for Maria, Casey's fiancée. Last week my mom joined a gym, and the trainer told her that although she didn't look a day older than fifty-two, because of all the stress she works under, she's actually ten years older on the inside. Cody is my brother, and "Nanny" is my beloved grandmother.

Hopefully, this information will fill in the many blanks left in the e-mail. (By the way, this is actually copied-and-pasted from my Inbox. My mother obviously didn't have time for trivial things like "Dear Lisa" or "Love, Mom." Maybe because it was time-stamped at 4:32 a.m.)

I was in a Christian bookstore yesterday in McKinney. They would like to do a book signing for your next book. Yes, I morphed into Nanny.

Here is my advice to you re: teenagers—just when you think you can't stand them another minute, grab some of your scrapbooks, jump in the car, and drive around the block and park. Look through those pictures and realize how short the time is. I think it will have the same effect as looking at a two-year-old asleep.

I hope this shower knocks it out of the ballpark. I want to make Casey proud.

I'm not taking any new clients until this summer and maybe not until September.

Introduction

I can't wait to see Cody on Sunday. He's so handsome.

I want to write a book about how to be sixty-two, look fifty-two on the outside, seem seventy-two on the inside, feel forty-two, act thirty-two, and make a million or two overnight in real estate.

I love Maria.

As you probably noticed, my mother lives life in shorthand. Her conversations are pithy and to the point. Her business dealings are swift and fierce. Her words are crisp and abrupt. Her wisdom is concise and potent, which makes her the perfect candidate to help me write *The Busy Grandma's Guide to Prayer.*

Today's grandma is not your mother's mother! She's like you—busy and tired and wise and worried and loving and dependent on God. There is one major difference between me and my mother: age. And with those years come a lifetime of experiences I've yet to have. The same is true of you. Along with those crinkles around your twinkling eyes, threads of gray in your hair, and more-to-love fluffiness around your middle, you've also gained invaluable, irreplaceable, incomparable wisdom. What a gift to your children and your grandchildren!

Many years ago I listened to an audiotape of a speaker stating his belief that the command to honor our father and mother was without an expiration date. I completely agree with him . . . now. I can't say I was fully on board until I had children of my own and grew up a little.

I've heard my own children cry out in frustration, "When

Introduction

I grow up, I'm not going to have to . . ." or, as recently as this morning, "After I turn eighteen, I'm going to . . ." The blank in the fill-in ellipses is, basically, "I'm going to do things my way, not my parent's way."

I remember thinking those same thoughts. But not anymore. One reason is, I consider God's words on the stone tablets to be as much a promise as a command. The rest of the verse in Exodus 20:12—the one that starts out, "Honor your father and your mother"—reads, "that your days may be long in the land that the LORD your God is giving you." It is a privilege to honor my mother, and when I do, my life is blessed.

God has given you, as a grandma, wisdom that I do not have, experiences that I have not faced, and an inner depth and breadth that can only come with time and maturity. These days, when my mother tells me to take my calcium, I rush to the drugstore, because she's trying to teach me something from her experience so I don't have to learn it the hard way.

As a teenager I didn't always listen to her: why in the world do I need to wash my face every single night? I didn't even always listen to her as a young adult: A retirement account? I want a house with a pool!

I don't know who's gotten smarter—her or me. I'm pretty sure I've just gotten enough smarter to realize that *she's* smarter. Now that I'm old enough to know better, I know that *she* knows better.

I gladly submit to her wisdom, and I'm thankful for her experience. Her age is a gift to me. As her only daughter, I'll rise to call her blessed so fast that it'll make my head spin. I will also call her friend. At this very moment I'm at her house, writing. She just offered to make me a cup of hot chocolate, and fifteen minutes ago the fresh flowers I ordered for her "just because" were delivered to her door. We are crazy about each other (emphasis on the word *crazy*).

With this book, we enter a new season of our relationship— one in which we are partners. I can't express how thrilled I was when she agreed to coauthor this book with me. I've always known my mother was a fabulous writer, and we've talked about writing a screenplay together. We just assumed our project would come after my children were grown and her millions were made.

What a gift this experience has been to me. What a gift her experience will be to you. By Day 1 of this guided prayer journal, I believe you'll feel just like I do about my mother. You'll consider her a friend and a partner. I know that her prayers for her spectacular grandchildren will also express your heart for your equally extraordinary grandchildren.

So, it is with great pride and honor that I introduce you to my remarkable mother, Gentry Coleman. May her words and prayers bless you and your family as much as they have blessed me and mine.

Gentry's Introduction

I wasn't fully prepared for the love I feel for my grandchildren. It never came in waves, as I had presumed it would, growing with each child and every passing year. Instead, it washed over me like a tsunami from the moment I met the first one, with a fresh flood overwhelming my heart at each subsequent birth.

I don't know how I expected to feel, but thinking about my grandchildren still takes my breath away. I think God gives us grandchildren so we can experience pure love—both for them and from them. Grandchildren don't care how old you are, how fat you are, or how rich or poor you are—they just accept you.

In turn, there's nothing quite like the unconditional love kids receive from a grandmother. In what other relationship can everything a child say be met with a sincere belly laugh or genuine amazement? Who but a grandma looks around to make sure everyone in the room caught the adorable words spoken by the young genius? Whom can a child count on at the conclusion of every recital for the heartfelt words, "You were the best one"? And it must be true, because Grandma said so! To whom does a child run after outright foolishness, looking for a defender to explain, "She's just a child" (even if she's a teenager)?

A grandmother holds a place like no other in a child's life. And no one this side of heaven can storm the gates of heaven on behalf of a child like a grandmother. She has passion, wisdom, insight, and experience; but most of all she has a laser-focused love for that particular child that no one else possesses quite as intensely.

I want this tsunami of emotion to flow through my prayers until they flood the crystal sea surrounding the throne of God and move His heart for my grandchildren.

All I need is the time.

"It gives me more time to pray for my grandchildren"— those were the words spoken by an older woman when asked what she enjoyed most about retirement. And they're words I've never forgotten. It's also the image I've carried in my mind and heart for all these years: I always assumed that by this age, I'd be sitting around in a rocking chair with plenty of time on my hands, spending hours lifting up my precious grandbabies in prayer, waiting for a Social Security check and a phone call from my sons. (I knew my daughter, Lisa, would have called me twice by noon.)

That, however, has not been my reality. The older I got, the more I realized that I probably would not share the lifestyle of grandmothers before me—or before divorces, second marriages, and credit cards. Many grandmothers like me in my generation are still working, dieting, and striving. Yet I've never forgotten what I really wanted to be doing—praying for my grandchildren.

But how? I'm busier than I've ever been. I thought life would slow down, but it has only gotten faster as my body slows down. I wake up tired before the craziness of the day even begins. I must spend my time preparing for the future until I'm too exhausted to enjoy today.

Don't get me wrong—I'm thankful for health and purpose and a reason to get up in the morning. It's just that I'd like to get up with a bit more spring in my step and have a bit more

Introduction

time to invest in the future beyond my future. I'd like to have the energy to pray for all that's on my heart and mind, especially my beloved grandchildren.

I know the power of prayer. I know the things I want to pray about. I know prayer changes lives. What I don't know is how to find the time. There doesn't seem to be enough hours in the day.

Then my daughter approached me about writing a book with her for grandmothers just like me—grandmas who want to pray for their grandchildren but don't know how to get started or, more precisely, how to get beyond just starting.

I began to see hope on the horizon for my prayer life when Lisa and I brainstormed and came up with six individual prayer focus topics. That was it: what I needed was to focus. I felt scattered. Throughout the day I prayed for things I thought about or worried about. I prayed if one of my grandchildren was taking a test or competing in some event. I prayed for my grandkids' relationships with their parents and siblings and friends. Which got me thinking, I should pray that they'll be able to stand up against peer pressure. Then I would think about all the dangers threatening my treasured grandchildren and pray for their safety, for their protection from strangers, and that they would use wisdom when surfing the Internet. The more I prayed, the more I knew I needed to pray more. I always came up lacking, feeling guilty, exhausted, and overwhelmed when I had barely begun.

I'd love to tarry in prayer, but that may have to wait a few more years. In the meantime, I don't want to keep putting prayer off because I can't spend hours interceding from my rocking chair. By breaking down all of my hopes, dreams, concerns, and desires for my grandchildren into these six main categories, I'm able to saturate their lives with passionate, powerful prayer in less than ten minutes a day.

Self

I've been around long enough to know that I can't do anything, even pray, without help. That's why I'm not ashamed to begin praying for my grandchildren by praying for myself. I ask for mercy, grace, and wisdom in how to pray. I pray for my health so I can have more time with my children and grandchildren—which means making time to exercise and eat right. I pray about my finances, my Bible study, and my work. It's not selfish to pray for yourself. God knows our needs, but it's important for us to give Him our concerns every day.

Adult Children

Is there any such thing? To me they're still just my children. I have so much hard-won wisdom that I want to impart to my grown children, but sometimes that just isn't my place any more. So I talk to God about all the things they need. I ask Him to protect them from credit-card debt and working too much and to help them see the importance of spending time with their children. I pray daily for their relationships with their spouses and children. I pray for healing from childhood traumas only I know about—and any I don't. I pray for their walk with the Lord. I pray for their protection against a world full of temptation and acceptance of sin.

Introduction

Grandchildren

This is easy in part because I've made enough mistakes with their parents to know how to pray for them. I know the importance of choosing the right friends and activities. I know the value of emotional protection and purity. I know drugs are everywhere. I know school is hard—and not just the academic part. So I start with their salvation and the salvation of their friends. I pray that they'll learn at an early age to take a firm stand when necessary. I pray they'll find their identity in Jesus. I find great joy in praying for my grandchildren!

Grandchildren's Future

God knows our future, and yet He gave us free will. I know my grandchildren's future will be determined largely by the choices they make. So I pray that they'll make no choice without consulting Him first. To some degree I've seen their future too: some things never change. So I can pray for their future families, future jobs, and even future retirement with some insight. But my deepest desire is that they will make a difference in the future and for the kingdom of God—that they will recognize their ability to reach the masses or the few. Of course, I want my grandchildren to have a smooth, easy life, free of heartache and pain. But I know that's not possible, so I pray that in difficult times to come, they'll run to the Counselor and Comforter.

Grandchildren's Character

I think my grandchildren are perfect just the way they are: I wouldn't change a thing about them. So when I pray about their character, I pray that they'll have Jesus's take on things. I pray that they'll seek His approval and depend on His Word to guide them. The fruit of the Spirit and other godly character traits can only be grown by the Master Gardener, so I look to Him to plant, cultivate, prune, and produce the character of Jesus within my grandchildren.

Children of the World

How can any grandmother not pray for these little lost souls? It's the only thing most of us can do for children of the world. Most of the topics in this area of focus are beyond the realm of our own experiences, so we have to pray for the things we see on TV or read about. I'm thankful for these resources because without them I wouldn't know about the extreme nature of these precious childrens' needs. We might not all be able to give financial aid, but we can give prayer aid.

Hopefully, these six areas of focus, each with twenty more narrowly focused topics throughout this book, will get you off to a good start—and help you along—as you pray for your beloved grandchildren. Remember, with just ten minutes of focused entreaty every day, you'll cover 120 far-reaching, deeply penetrating, eternal-life-changing areas of prayer. Imagine the impact such a few minutes can have on the lives of your family!

I won't be surprised if you occasionally find pockets of time for extended prayer. So with that in mind, we've included plenty of room for you to make this prayer journal more personal. Use the blank lines however works best for you. You may want

Introduction

to write the names of each of your grandchildren beside the topics on which you feel particularly impressed to pray for them. Write out your prayer, and don't forget to come back and jot down a note of praise for God's answer. This little book you hold in your hands can become an heirloom—just think what an invaluable inheritance you'll create as you make this journal your own.

Day 1

Self

☕ **Prayer Focus**—Health

📖 Scripture Inspiration

Beloved, I pray that you may prosper in all things and be in health, just as your soul prospers (3 John 2 NKJV).

☉ Praying the Word

Thank You, Lord, that You love me and desire to see me physically, emotionally, and financially healthy and prosperous. I receive these gifts from Your hand.

🌸 Prayer Prompt

Jesus, I desire to live a long and healthy life. Give me strength and comfort in this wonderful but aging body with which You've blessed me. Please heal me specifically in this area: _____. I also pray for a sharp mind and a peaceful heart. Allow me to have all that I need to fulfill Your plans for my life and to have the energy and ability to keep up with my grandchildren.

Prayer Focus _____

Scripture Inspiration

_____
_____
_____
_____

Praying the Word

_____
_____
_____
_____
_____

Prayer Prompt

_____
_____
_____
_____
_____
_____
_____
_____
_____

3

Day 1
Adult Children

☕ **Prayer Focus**—Marriage

📖 Scripture Inspiration

They are no longer two but one flesh. What therefore God has joined together, let not man separate (Matthew 19:6).

☉ Praying the Word

Draw my children and their spouses together in unity. Keep them close, and don't allow anything to come between them.

❀ Prayer Prompt

Almighty God, I cry out to You on behalf of my children and ask You to protect them from the enemy and all that he uses to break up marriages. I pray they will not only remain married for a lifetime but that they will also grow more united and in love with each other through each passing year. May they pass on a legacy of commitment and faithfulness to my grandchildren.

Prayer Focus _____

Scripture Inspiration

_____

_____

_____

_____

Praying the Word

_____

_____

_____

_____

_____

_____

Prayer Prompt

_____

_____

_____

_____

_____

_____

_____

_____

_____

_____

Day 1

Grandchildren

☕ **Prayer Focus**—Physical Safety

📖Scripture Inspiration

The Lord will keep you from all evil; he will keep your life (Psalm 121:7).

☉ Praying the Word

Thank You, Lord, for protecting my grandchildren from harm and allowing them to live out the fullness of the days You've planned for them.

🌸Prayer Prompt

Almighty God, place a hedge of protection around my dear grandchildren. Assign angels to guard them wherever they go, all day and all night. Keep them from accidents, attacks from the enemy, or harm in any way. Go before them and clear their paths, making them straight and safe.

Prayer Focus _____

Scripture Inspiration

_____

_____

_____

_____

Praying the Word

_____

_____

_____

_____

_____

Prayer Prompt

_____

_____

_____

_____

_____

_____

_____

_____

Day 1
Grandchildren's Future

☕ **Prayer Focus**—Children

📖 Scripture Inspiration

Each generation can set its hope anew on God, remembering his glorious miracles, and obeying his commands (Psalm 78:7 NLT).

☉ Praying the Word

Lord, I pray that my great-grandchildren will make a personal commitment to worship and obey you so that they, in turn, may pass on a godly heritage to each generation of our family.

🌸 Prayer Prompt

Thank You in advance for great-grandchildren and great-great-grandchildren! Allow me to go so far as to pray for the blessing of all of my offspring until Your return. May each and every child who carries my DNA serve You from a heart of adoration and walk in faith all the days of their lives.

Prayer Focus _____

Scripture Inspiration

_____
_____
_____
_____

Praying the Word

_____
_____
_____
_____
_____

Prayer Prompt

_____
_____
_____
_____
_____
_____
_____
_____

Day 1

Grandchildren's Character

☕ **Prayer Focus**—Gratitude

📖 **Scripture Inspiration**

Let the word of Christ dwell in you richly, . . . singing psalms and hymns and spiritual songs, with thankfulness in your hearts to God (Colossians 3:16).

🕙 **Praying the Word**

Lord, give my grandchildren grateful hearts that overflow with praise.

🌸 **Prayer Prompt**

It's difficult in this age of abundance to foster gratitude and contentment in young people. So I'm asking You to cultivate a spirit of thankfulness in my grandchildren.

Children of the World

☕ **Prayer Focus**—Sexually Abused

📖 **Scripture Inspiration**

I have heard your prayer; I have seen your tears. Behold, I will heal you (2 Kings 20:5).

🕙 **Praying the Word**

Father, You hear the cry of each sexually abused child. Heal them by Your grace and power.

🌸 **Prayer Prompt**

Comfort, heal, and deliver each child who has been sexually abused. Show them Your tender love and victorious plan for their lives.

🍵 Prayer Focus _____

📖 Scripture Inspiration

_____
_____

🕥 Praying the Word

_____
_____

🌸 Prayer Prompt

_____
_____
_____

🍵 Prayer Focus _____

📖 Scripture Inspiration

_____
_____

🕥 Praying the Word

_____
_____

🌸 Prayer Prompt

_____
_____
_____

11

Day 2

Self

📖 Scripture Inspiration

Like arrows in the hand of a warrior are the children of one's youth (Psalm 127:4).

☉ Praying the Word

Lord, give me wisdom in dealing with my adult children so that I may prayerfully release them to reach the goals and purposes for which You created them.

❀ Prayer Prompt

Thank You, Lord, for my children. Grant us good, healthy, life-giving communication with each other. Give us a close friendship based on mutual respect. May this relationship be marked by truth, joy, forgiveness, and peace. Help me convey my love to each child in ways he or she will be able to receive. Do not allow the enemy to destroy this most treasured of relationships.

Prayer Focus _____

Scripture Inspiration

_____
_____
_____
_____

Praying the Word

_____
_____
_____
_____
_____
_____

Prayer Prompt

_____
_____
_____
_____
_____
_____
_____
_____
_____

Day 2
Adult Children

☕ **Prayer Focus**—Parenting

📖 Scripture Inspiration

Train up a child in the way he should go; even when he is old he will not depart from it (Proverbs 22:6).

☉ Praying the Word

Father, enable my children to rear their children according to Your ways. Keep them following You all the days of their lives.

❀ Prayer Prompt

Grant an extra measure of wisdom, grace, patience, mercy, and love to my children as they endeavor to raise children in these tumultuous times. Give them insight, and anoint them to shape and mold each child in accordance with the gifts You've already placed within each one. Show them how to express love through a balance of discipline and grace.

Prayer Focus _____

Scripture Inspiration

_____

_____

_____

_____

Praying the Word

_____

_____

_____

_____

_____

Prayer Prompt

_____

_____

_____

_____

_____

_____

_____

_____

_____

Day 2

Grandchildren

Prayer Focus—School

Scripture Inspiration

The heart of him who has understanding seeks knowledge, but the mouths of fools feed on folly (Proverbs 15:14).

Praying the Word

Lord, give my grandchildren a desire to learn and a distaste for foolishness.

Prayer Prompt

Help my grandchildren to do well in school. Give them godly friendships and favor with their teachers. Grant them a teachable spirit and a love for knowledge. Bless them with quick minds and an ability to comprehend instruction. Develop in them critical thinking skills and a Christian worldview. Enable them to discern truth, and let them be a witness for You in their classrooms.

Prayer Focus _____

Scripture Inspiration

_____

_____

_____

_____

Praying the Word

_____

_____

_____

_____

_____

Prayer Prompt

_____

_____

_____

_____

_____

_____

_____

_____

_____

Day 2
Grandchildren's Future

☕ **Prayer Focus**—Vocation

📖 Scripture Inspiration

Do you see a man skillful in his work? He will stand before kings; he will not stand before obscure men (Proverbs 22:29).

☉ Praying the Word

God, give my grandchildren the ability and desire for excellence in whatever they do, and may they find favor through their work.

❀ Prayer Prompt

Help my grandchildren to discover the work You've created them to do. Don't let them settle for just good employment or adequate pay. Let them find deep joy and satisfaction, knowing they're fulfilling their God-ordained destiny. Whether their job be glamorous or humble, give them a sense of high calling and the assurance that they're exactly where You want them to be, doing what You created them to do.

Prayer Focus _____

Scripture Inspiration

_____

_____

_____

_____

Praying the Word

_____

_____

_____

_____

_____

_____

Prayer Prompt

_____

_____

_____

_____

_____

_____

_____

_____

_____

Day 2

Grandchildren's Character

Prayer Focus—Selflessness

Scripture Inspiration

Do not use your freedom as an opportunity for the flesh, but through love serve one another (Galatians 5:13).

Praying the Word

Father, mold my grandchildren's hearts into those of selfless servants.

Prayer Prompt

You've given my grandchildren so much; let that prompt them to give to others. Guard them against selfishness. Grant them eyes to see needs and ready hands to meet those needs.

Children of the World

Prayer Focus—Hunger

Scripture Inspiration

Those who were hungry have ceased to hunger (1 Samuel 2:5).

Praying the Word

God, I look to You to provide food for the hungry children of the world.

Prayer Prompt

You fed five thousand men with five loaves and two fish, and You still can do miracles. Fill the bellies and the souls of children with bread from Your hand.

🍵 Prayer Focus _____

📖 Scripture Inspiration

_____

_____

🕊 Praying the Word

_____

_____

🌸 Prayer Prompt

_____

_____

_____

🍵 Prayer Focus _____

📖 Scripture Inspiration

_____

_____

🕊 Praying the Word

_____

_____

🌸 Prayer Prompt

_____

_____

_____

Day 3

Self

☕ **Prayer Focus**—Marriage

📖 Scripture Inspiration

Has not the LORD made them one? In flesh and spirit they are his. And why one? Because he was seeking godly offspring (Malachi 2:15 NIV).

☺ Praying the Word

Draw my husband and me closer together in every way. Allow us to be a witness of Your love to our children and grandchildren, that we might pass on a godly heritage.

🌸 Prayer Prompt

Father, I pray for a marriage that is ever growing. Delight my husband and me with new discoveries and fresh reasons to fall in love all over again. Teach him how to love me in ways that touch my soul. Show me how to respect him in such a way that he has the confidence to be everything You created him to be. Help us to guard our hearts so the enemy is unable to creep in and divide our home.

☕ Prayer Focus _____

📖 Scripture Inspiration

_____
_____
_____
_____

🕙 Praying the Word

_____
_____
_____
_____
_____
_____

🌸 Prayer Prompt

_____
_____
_____
_____
_____
_____
_____
_____
_____

Day 3
Adult Children

☕ **Prayer Focus**—Work

📖 **Scripture Inspiration**

Let the favor of the LORD our God be upon us, and establish the work of our hands upon us; yes, establish the work of our hands (Psalm 90:17).

☉ **Praying the Word**

Lord, bless my children and give them meaningful work to accomplish. Anoint them to live out their calling and purpose.

🌸 **Prayer Prompt**

Please grant my children the privilege of loving what they do. May it be so fulfilling to them that they can barely call it work. Allow them to make an eternal difference in the job You've assigned them in this season of their lives.

Prayer Focus _____

Scripture Inspiration

_____
_____
_____
_____

Praying the Word

_____
_____
_____
_____
_____
_____

Prayer Prompt

_____
_____
_____
_____
_____
_____
_____
_____
_____

Day 3
Grandchildren

☕ **Prayer Focus**—Friends

📖 Scripture Inspiration

Iron sharpens iron, and one man sharpens another (Proverbs 27:17).

☉ Praying the Word

Bless my grandchildren with friendships that are mutually strengthening.

❀ Prayer Prompt

Father, handpick the friends with whom You surround my grandchildren. Place godly young people, with hearts that seek and follow Your ways, in the positions of closest impact. Bless my grandchildren with best friends with whom they can share their hearts, lives, and lots of laughs. Teach them how to be good and loyal friends to others.

☕ Prayer Focus _____

📖 Scripture Inspiration

_____

_____

_____

_____

🕓 Praying the Word

_____

_____

_____

_____

_____

🌸 Prayer Prompt

_____

_____

_____

_____

_____

_____

_____

_____

_____

Day 3
Grandchildren's Future

☕ **Prayer Focus**—Spiritual Gifts

📖 **Scripture Inspiration**

Having gifts that differ according to the grace given to us, let us use them (Romans 12:6).

🕐 **Praying the Word**

Thank You, Lord, for placing specific gifts and talents within each of my grandchildren. Bring these unique attributes to the surface, and open doors of opportunity for my amazing grandchildren to exercise them for Your glory.

🌸 **Prayer Prompt**

Open my eyes to see the treasures You've placed within my grandchildren. Open their eyes, as well, to recognize the spiritual gifts You've given them. Encourage them to operate in these gifts from an early age. May they sense a deep joy and peace when they use their gifts to serve You.

Prayer Focus _____

Scripture Inspiration

_____

_____

_____

_____

Praying the Word

_____

_____

_____

_____

_____

_____

Prayer Prompt

_____

_____

_____

_____

_____

_____

_____

_____

_____

Day 3

Grandchildren's Character

☕ **Prayer Focus**—Diligence

📖 **Scripture Inspiration**
The plans of the diligent lead surely to abundance (Proverbs 21:5).

🕙 **Praying the Word**
God, establish in my grandchildren a solid work ethic.

🌸 **Prayer Prompt**
Give my grandchildren the privilege of enjoying a job well done. Let them experience hard work and the satisfaction of taking healthy pride in their accomplishments.

Children of the World

☕ **Prayer Focus**—Homeless

📖 **Scripture Inspiration**
Some wandered in desert wastes, finding no way to a city to dwell in; hungry and thirsty, their soul fainted within them. Then they cried to the Lord in their trouble, and he delivered them from their distress (Psalm 107:4–6).

🕙 **Praying the Word**
Lord, rescue children who are hopelessly and homelessly wandering the streets.

🌸 **Prayer Prompt**
Hide them under the shelter of Your wings. Provide safety and warmth for each child who is crying alone, without a place to call home.

☕ Prayer Focus _____

📖 Scripture Inspiration

_____

_____

🕉 Praying the Word

_____

_____

🌸 Prayer Prompt

_____

_____

_____

☕ Prayer Focus _____

📖 Scripture Inspiration

_____

_____

🕉 Praying the Word

_____

_____

🌸 Prayer Prompt

_____

_____

_____

Day 4

Self

📖 Scripture Inspiration

She opens her mouth with wisdom, and the teaching of kindness is on her tongue (Proverbs 31:26).

☾ Praying the Word

God, fill my heart with wise words, and teach me how to share Your wisdom with a gentle and loving spirit.

❀ Prayer Prompt

Lord, often I don't know what to say or what to do. Please give me wisdom. Open my ears to hear Your voice directing me and correcting me. I desire wisdom, especially in regard to my grandchildren. Help me to know what to say and, equally important, what not to say. Make me a vessel filled with words of wisdom from above.

Prayer Focus _____

Scripture Inspiration

_____

_____

_____

_____

Praying the Word

_____

_____

_____

_____

_____

Prayer Prompt

_____

_____

_____

_____

_____

_____

_____

_____

_____

Day 4
Adult Children

☕ **Prayer Focus**—Children

📖 **Scripture Inspiration**

Children are a heritage from the LORD, the fruit of the womb a reward (Psalm 127:3).

☉ **Praying the Word**

Thank You, Lord, for honoring my children with the gift of having children of their own.

🌼 **Prayer Prompt**

Place a fresh wave of love and gratefulness in my children's hearts today for the privilege of being parents. Give them a vision for leading their children to salvation and a life of service for Your kingdom. Grant them deep, meaningful relationships with each of their children—and time to enjoy these fleeting years.

☕ Prayer Focus _____

📖 Scripture Inspiration

_____

_____

_____

_____

🕥 Praying the Word

_____

_____

_____

_____

_____

_____

🌿 Prayer Prompt

_____

_____

_____

_____

_____

_____

_____

_____

_____

Day 4

Grandchildren

☕ **Prayer Focus**—Emotional Protection

📖 Scripture Inspiration

He will command his angels concerning you to guard you in all your ways (Psalm 91:11).

☉ Praying the Word

Commission angels to protect my grandchildren on all sides—inside and out.

🌸 Prayer Prompt

God, guard my grandchildren's hearts, minds, souls, and spirits as well as their bodies. Protect them from careless or angry words. Deliver them from bullies and cliques. Teach them how to deal with their emotions in healthy ways. Comfort them with the presence of Your Holy Spirit when they are alone with painful or confusing feelings. Erase from their minds the lies spoken to them by the enemy, others, or even themselves. Speak the truth of Your love loud and clear to their hearts, and bring wholeness.

Prayer Focus _____

Scripture Inspiration

_____

_____

_____

_____

Praying the Word

_____

_____

_____

_____

_____

_____

Prayer Prompt

_____

_____

_____

_____

_____

_____

_____

_____

_____

Day 4
Grandchildren's Future

☕ **Prayer Focus**—Spouse

📖 Scripture Inspiration

You have been set apart as holy to the LORD your God, and he has chosen you to be his own special treasure (Deuteronomy 14:2 NLT).

☺ Praying the Word

Lord, give my grandchildren godly spouses who have been chosen especially for them.

❀ Prayer Prompt

Wherever my grandchildren's future spouses are right now in this world, I lift them up before Your throne. Deliver them from the evil one, and keep them close to You. Draw them into a personal relationship with You. Teach them the importance of submitting to their parents. Keep them pure and set apart for You and their future marriage.

Prayer Focus _____

Scripture Inspiration

_____

_____

_____

_____

Praying the Word

_____

_____

_____

_____

_____

_____

Prayer Prompt

_____

_____

_____

_____

_____

_____

_____

_____

_____

_____

Day 4

Grandchildren's Character

☕ **Prayer Focus**—Courage

📖 **Scripture Inspiration**
Wait for the Lord; be strong, and let your heart take courage (Psalm 27:14).

🕙 **Praying the Word**
Lord, teach my grandchildren to trust You in all situations.

❀ **Prayer Prompt**
May my grandchildren have full confidence in Your ability to equip, deliver, empower, lead, and defend them. Make them courageous leaders in their generation.

Children of the World

☕ **Prayer Focus**—Divorce

📖 **Scripture Inspiration**
Can a mother forget her nursing child? Can she feel no love for a child she has borne? But even if that were possible, I would not forget you (Isaiah 49:15 NLT).

🕙 **Praying the Word**
God, thank You for Your promise that even if others leave us, You will always remember and love us.

❀ **Prayer Prompt**
Comfort and heal the many children who are victims of divorce. Enable them to trust and love in spite of their pain. Fix their eyes on You.

🍵 Prayer Focus _____

📖 Scripture Inspiration

_____

_____

🕐 Praying the Word

_____

_____

🌸 Prayer Prompt

_____

_____

_____

🍵 Prayer Focus _____

📖 Scripture Inspiration

_____

_____

🕐 Praying the Word

_____

_____

🌸 Prayer Prompt

_____

_____

_____

Day 5

Self

📖 Scripture Inspiration

Grandchildren are the crown of the aged, and the glory of children is their fathers (Proverbs 17:6).

☉ Praying the Word

What a glorious privilege to be a grandmother! Thank You, Lord, for the honor.

❀ Prayer Prompt

Let me start by telling You how grateful I am for these grandchildren. What a joy! I know there is a special place in a child's life that only a grandmother can fill. Use me in a profound way to love unconditionally, encourage extravagantly, and pray powerfully. Give me both quantity and quality of time with each of my grandchildren, and may my touch make an eternal difference.

Prayer Focus _____

Scripture Inspiration

_____

_____

_____

_____

Praying the Word

_____

_____

_____

_____

_____

Prayer Prompt

_____

_____

_____

_____

_____

_____

_____

_____

_____

_____

Day 5
Adult Children

☕ **Prayer Focus**—Protection

📖 Scripture Inspiration

He will deliver you from the snare of the fowler and from the deadly pestilence. He will cover you with his pinions, and under his wings you will find refuge; his faithfulness is a shield and buckler (Psalm 91:3–4).

☉ Praying the Word

Thank You, God, for Your faithfulness to protect, defend, cover, and deliver my children from anything that would come against them or their family.

🌸 Prayer Prompt

I must confess that I often worry about the safety of my children and grandchildren. Today I choose to believe that they are in Your strong, powerful, and loving hands. Keep them safe from all harm, and deliver them from the evil one. Thank You for this assurance and the promises in Your Word.

☕ Prayer Focus _____

📖 Scripture Inspiration

_____

_____

_____

_____

☽ Praying the Word

_____

_____

_____

_____

_____

🌸 Prayer Prompt

_____

_____

_____

_____

_____

_____

_____

_____

_____

Day 5
Grandchildren

☕ **Prayer Focus**—Church

📖 Scripture Inspiration

Teach me your way, O LORD, that I may walk in your truth;
unite my heart to fear your name (Psalm 86:11).

☉ Praying the Word

Father, through Your church, instruct my grandchildren
in Your ways, that they might walk in submission to Your
Lordship with their whole hearts.

✿ Prayer Prompt

Give my grandchildren loving and anointed Sunday-
school teachers and youth leaders. Put a love for the
house of God and family of believers deep within their
hearts from an early age. May their best friends be ones
they make at church. I pray they will be able to say along
with David that one day in Your courts is better than a
thousand elsewhere.

Prayer Focus _____

Scripture Inspiration

_____
_____
_____
_____

Praying the Word

_____
_____
_____
_____
_____
_____

Prayer Prompt

_____
_____
_____
_____
_____
_____
_____
_____
_____

Day 5
Grandchildren's Future

☕ **Prayer Focus**—Ministry

📖 Scripture Inspiration

You are a chosen race, a royal priesthood, a holy nation, a people for his own possession, that you may proclaim the excellencies of him who called you out of darkness into his marvelous light (1 Peter 2:9).

☉ Praying the Word

God, set my grandchildren apart for Your high calling and purposes, that others might see them and be drawn to You.

🌸 Prayer Prompt

I pray that my grandchildren would see their lives as ministry. Regardless of their vocation, or even their service in the church, help them to understand that they are witnesses for You every day. Show them specifically where and how they can serve You, and empower them to step out and be used for Your glory.

Prayer Focus _____

Scripture Inspiration

_____

_____

_____

_____

Praying the Word

_____

_____

_____

_____

_____

_____

Prayer Prompt

_____

_____

_____

_____

_____

_____

_____

_____

_____

Day 5

Grandchildren's Character

☕ **Prayer Focus**—Worship

📖 **Scripture Inspiration**

They said to him, "Do you hear what these are saying?" And Jesus said to them, "Yes; have you never read, 'Out of the mouths of infants and nursing babies you have prepared praise'?" (Matthew 21:16).

Praying the Word

☉ Let worship well up within my grandchildren.

Prayer Prompt

🌸 God, give my grandchildren a glimpse of Your holiness so that spontaneous praise will spring from their lips and their lives. May everything they do be an offering of worship to You.

Children of the World

☕ **Prayer Focus**—Drug Addiction

📖 **Scripture Inspiration**

I have heard your prayer; I have seen your tears. Behold, I will heal you (2 Kings 20:5).

☉ **Praying the Word**

Father, set Your children free from addiction to drugs.

🌸 **Prayer Prompt**

Break the bonds that hold so many children to dependence on drugs. When they cry out to You, answer them with supernatural power and deliverance.

☕ Prayer Focus _____

📖 Scripture Inspiration

_____

_____

🕑 Praying the Word

_____

_____

❀ Prayer Prompt

_____

_____

_____

☕ Prayer Focus _____

📖 Scripture Inspiration

_____

_____

🕑 Praying the Word

_____

_____

❀ Prayer Prompt

_____

_____

_____

51

Day 6

Self

📖 Scripture Inspiration

For this reason I bow my knees before the Father, from whom every family in heaven and on earth is named, that according to the riches of his glory he may grant you to be strengthened with power through his Spirit in your inner being (Ephesians 3:14–16).

☉ Praying the Word

Heavenly Father, I'm glad You came up with the idea of family. I lift up all my relatives to You and ask that You would strengthen each of us with Your power, that we might radiate Your glorious riches to the world.

🌸 Prayer Prompt

Bless my family: father, mother, sisters, brothers, aunts, uncles, nieces, nephews, children, and grandchildren. Your storehouse contains enough riches to pour out abundantly on each of us. My desire is for every member of my family to know You intimately, walk with You daily, and serve You faithfully. Draw us closer to You and to each other for Your glory.

🍵 Prayer Focus _____

📖 Scripture Inspiration

_____

_____

_____

_____

🕐 Praying the Word

_____

_____

_____

_____

_____

🌸 Prayer Prompt

_____

_____

_____

_____

_____

_____

_____

_____

Day 6
Adult Children

📖 Scripture Inspiration

If any of you lacks wisdom, let him ask God, who gives generously to all without reproach, and it will be given him (James 1:5).

☉ Praying the Word

God, I am asking on behalf of my children for an abundance of wisdom to be granted to them in liberal measure.

❀ Prayer Prompt

We all need wisdom these days, but never more than when we're attempting to train children in the way they should go. Give my children the supernatural wisdom to know how to teach Your laws in practical ways. Remind them to call out to You when they don't know what to do. Thank You that You're already there, waiting to answer.

🍵 Prayer Focus _____

📖 Scripture Inspiration

_____

_____

_____

_____

🕓 Praying the Word

_____

_____

_____

_____

_____

🌼 Prayer Prompt

_____

_____

_____

_____

_____

_____

_____

_____

_____

Day 6
Grandchildren

Prayer Focus—Salvation

Scripture Inspiration

If you confess with your mouth that Jesus is Lord and believe in your heart that God raised him from the dead, you will be saved (Romans 10:9).

Praying the Word

Jesus, I pray that my grandchildren will call You Lord and put their faith in You as their risen savior.

Prayer Prompt

Even more than my joy the day they were born, I anticipate the joy of seeing my grandchildren born again. Prepare the soil of their hearts to receive the seed of Your Word with gladness. May the roots of truth go deep and bear much fruit for eternity.

Prayer Focus _____

Scripture Inspiration

_____

_____

_____

_____

Praying the Word

_____

_____

_____

_____

_____

_____

Prayer Prompt

_____

_____

_____

_____

_____

_____

_____

_____

Day 6
Grandchildren's Future

☕ **Prayer Focus**—Wise Stewards

📖 Scripture Inspiration

Keep your life free from love of money, and be content with what you have, for he has said, "I will never leave you nor forsake you" (Hebrews 13:5).

☉ Praying the Word

Father, I pray that my grandchildren will trust in You so completely that they aren't even tempted to look elsewhere for happiness.

🌸 Prayer Prompt

I do pray that You'll provide abundantly for my grandchildren and their families. I know that is Your will. At the same time, I pray that they will know contentment in whatever financial state they're in. Help them establish wise stewardship habits from the beginning. Keep them free from debt, faithful regarding obligations, balanced in spending, and generous in giving.

🍵 Prayer Focus _____

📖 Scripture Inspiration

_____

_____

_____

_____

🕙 Praying the Word

_____

_____

_____

_____

_____

🌼 Prayer Prompt

_____

_____

_____

_____

_____

_____

_____

_____

Day 6

Grandchildren's Character

☕ **Prayer Focus**—Discernment

📖 **Scripture Inspiration**

A wise man's heart discerns both time and judgment (Ecclesiastes 8:5 NKJV).

🕙 **Praying the Word**

Father, grant my grandchildren the wisdom to know what to do and when to do it in any given situation.

🌸 **Prayer Prompt**

Teach my grandchildren how to discern rightly in this age of blurred boundaries. Show them when the wisdom of the world is foolishness to You—and vice versa.

Children of the World

☕ **Prayer Focus**—Gangs

📖 **Scripture Inspiration**

My times are in your hand; rescue me from the hand of my enemies (Psalm 31:15).

🕙 **Praying the Word**

God, rescue children from those who would lead them down a path of destruction.

🌸 **Prayer Prompt**

You are more powerful than any gang. Have mercy on the children, and lead them to a better life. Protect them from their enemies, and be their defender.

Prayer Focus _____

Scripture Inspiration

_____

_____

Praying the Word

_____

_____

Prayer Prompt

_____

_____

_____

Prayer Focus _____

Scripture Inspiration

_____

_____

Praying the Word

_____

_____

Prayer Prompt

_____

_____

_____

Day 7

Self

📖 Scripture Inspiration

Oil and perfume make the heart glad, and the sweetness of a friend comes from his earnest counsel (Proverbs 27:9).

☾ Praying the Word

Lord, I'm so glad that You've blessed me with good friends. They are a sweet gift from Your hand. May my friends and I speak the truth in love and encourage one another sincerely.

🌸 Prayer Prompt

I lift up each of my friends to You and ask You to bless them today with good health, invigorating purpose, healthy relationships, and a personal word from You to their spirit. Show me how to be a faithful and life-giving friend. Lord, would You also grant me friendship with my grandchildren? I want them to want to spend time with me, talk to me, and trust in me, not only as a grandmother but also as a friend.

Prayer Focus _____

Scripture Inspiration

_____

_____

_____

_____

Praying the Word

_____

_____

_____

_____

_____

_____

Prayer Prompt

_____

_____

_____

_____

_____

_____

_____

_____

Day 7
Adult Children

☕ **Prayer Focus**—Church

📖 **Scripture Inspiration**

They were enrolled with all their little children, their wives, their sons, and their daughters, the whole assembly, for they were faithful in keeping themselves holy (2 Chronicles 31:18).

🔆 **Praying the Word**

Give my children a Bible-believing, faith-based, set-apart church they can truly call home, with a body of believers they can call family.

🌸 **Prayer Prompt**

Father, I pray that my children and their families will be actively involved in a local church. Knit their hearts together with those of other believers, and give them true community that comes from deep fellowship and quality time spent together. Anoint their pastor to feed their spirits from Your Word.

Prayer Focus _____

Scripture Inspiration

_____

_____

_____

_____

Praying the Word

_____

_____

_____

_____

_____

_____

Prayer Prompt

_____

_____

_____

_____

_____

_____

_____

_____

Day 7
Grandchildren

☕ **Prayer Focus**—Purity

📖 Scripture Inspiration

Let no one despise you for your youth, but set the believers an example in speech, in conduct, in love, in faith, in purity (1 Timothy 4:12).

☾ Praying the Word

From the very beginning give my grandchildren a desire to walk in holiness and purity in thought, word, and deed.

🌸 Prayer Prompt

Father, purify my grandchildren's hearts, because I know that whatever is in the heart will be manifested in word and deed. Keep them pure not only sexually but also in their "thought lives" and in their speech. Protect them from the evil that bombards their senses on every side. May they have a godly innocence all the days of their lives.

Prayer Focus _____

Scripture Inspiration

_____

_____

_____

_____

Praying the Word

_____

_____

_____

_____

_____

_____

Prayer Prompt

_____

_____

_____

_____

_____

_____

_____

_____

_____

Day 7
Grandchildren's Future

☕ **Prayer Focus**—Goals

📖 Scripture Inspiration

Commit your work to the LORD, and your plans will be established (Proverbs 16:3).

☉ Praying the Word

Father, teach my grandchildren the wisdom of submitting their hopes and dreams to You.

🌸 Prayer Prompt

Place Your desires in my grandchildren's hearts. May they want the things You want and seek that which is pleasing to You. With their hearts submitted to You, I pray they will set goals in light of the knowledge that nothing is impossible with You.

Prayer Focus _____

Scripture Inspiration

_____

_____

_____

_____

Praying the Word

_____

_____

_____

_____

_____

Prayer Prompt

_____

_____

_____

_____

_____

_____

_____

_____

_____

Day 7

Grandchildren's Character

☕ **Prayer Focus**—Obedience

📖 **Scripture Inspiration**

Children, obey your parents in everything, for this pleases the Lord (Colossians 3:20).

🕓 **Praying the Word**

Father, I pray that my grandchildren would obey their parents out of respect for them and, more importantly, out of love for You.

❀ **Prayer Prompt**

Help my grandchildren to see the wisdom, safety, and freedom that comes from obeying their parents. I pray that they will obey from a submissive heart and with a right attitude.

Children of the World

☕ **Prayer Focus**—War

📖 **Scripture Inspiration**

Defend the cause of the poor of the people, give deliverance to the children of the needy, and crush the oppressor (Psalm 72:4).

🕓 **Praying the Word**

Father, keep Your eyes on the tiniest victims of war and protect them.

❀ **Prayer Prompt**

In the midst of chaos and confusion, give them peace that passes understanding and a deep conviction that You are ultimately in control, and they are safe with You.

🍵 Prayer Focus _____

📖 Scripture Inspiration

_____

_____

🕐 Praying the Word

_____

_____

🌸 Prayer Prompt

_____

_____

_____

🍵 Prayer Focus _____

📖 Scripture Inspiration

_____

_____

🕐 Praying the Word

_____

_____

🌸 Prayer Prompt

_____

_____

_____

Day 8

Self

📖 Scripture Inspiration

The whole body, joined and held together by every joint with which it is equipped, when each part is working properly, makes the body grow so that it builds itself up in love (Ephesians 4:16).

☉ Praying the Word

Lord, show me my place in the body of Christ. Fill me with Your love, and work through me that I might bless the family of God.

❁ Prayer Prompt

Give me opportunities to serve You by serving Your body. Anoint me for the work you've called me to do. Open my eyes to see opportunities for ministry every day. Remind me never to get so busy that I can't take advantage of "chance encounters" and "interruptions" that are, in reality, divine appointments from You. Help me to remember that my role as a grandma is a ministry too.

Prayer Focus _____

Scripture Inspiration

_____

_____

_____

_____

Praying the Word

_____

_____

_____

_____

_____

Prayer Prompt

_____

_____

_____

_____

_____

_____

_____

_____

_____

Day 8
Adult Children

☕ **Prayer Focus**—Priorities

📖 **Scripture Inspiration**

Seek first the kingdom of God and his righteousness, and all these things will be added to you (Matthew 6:33).

☽ **Praying the Word**

Father, keep my children's eyes focused on You above all else. Help them to trust You for all their needs and to know they will find those needs met in You.

🌸 **Prayer Prompt**

Give my children a vision of their lives from Your perspective. Help them to see what is truly important, and enable them to invest their time, resources, and affections in those things which are of eternal value. As they pursue a relationship with You, first and foremost, and then focus on their families, help them to trust You to take care of all the rest.

Prayer Focus _____

Scripture Inspiration

_____

_____

_____

_____

Praying the Word

_____

_____

_____

_____

_____

Prayer Prompt

_____

_____

_____

_____

_____

_____

_____

_____

Day 8
Grandchildren

☕ **Prayer Focus**—Health

📖 Scripture Inspiration

He himself bore our sins in his body on the tree, that we might die to sin and live to righteousness. By his wounds you have been healed (1 Peter 2:24).

☉ Praying the Word

Thank You, Jesus, for completing on the cross the work of my grandchildren's salvation and healing.

🌸 Prayer Prompt

Please keep my grandchildren healthy. Protect them from accidents, diseases, illnesses, and injuries. When they get sick, strengthen their immune systems to bring healing. Should they require medical attention, give the doctors wisdom and anoint them to care for my precious grandchildren. Thank You for Your provision of healing through both natural and supernatural means.

Prayer Focus _____

Scripture Inspiration

_____

_____

_____

_____

Praying the Word

_____

_____

_____

_____

_____

_____

Prayer Prompt

_____

_____

_____

_____

_____

_____

_____

_____

_____

_____

Day 8
Grandchildren's Future

☕ **Prayer Focus**—Family Relationships

📖 Scripture Inspiration

Believe in the Lord Jesus, and you will be saved, you and your household (Acts 16:31).

☉ Praying the Word

Father, I pray that my grandchildren will be surrounded by a family of believers all the days of their lives.

🌸 Prayer Prompt

From in-laws to stepfamilies, distant relatives to closest relations, I pray for peace and unity in all my grandchildren's future family relationships. May they enjoy the fellowship of their spouses' families and benefit from the bond of their own blood relatives. Anoint my grandchildren to be a "touch point" for You within their extended families.

🍵 Prayer Focus _____

📖 Scripture Inspiration

_____

_____

_____

_____

🕙 Praying the Word

_____

_____

_____

_____

_____

🌸 Prayer Prompt

_____

_____

_____

_____

_____

_____

_____

_____

_____

Day 8

Grandchildren's Character

☕ **Prayer Focus**—Love

📖 **Scripture Inspiration**
We love because he first loved us (1 John 4:19).

🕐 **Praying the Word**
Lord, fill my grandchildren with Your love so they can share it with the world.

🌸 **Prayer Prompt**
May my grandchildren's character be marked by Your selfless, gracious, joyful love. And let others sense Your love shining through them.

Children of the World

☕ **Prayer Focus**—Orphans

📖 **Scripture Inspiration**
Even if my father and mother abandon me, the LORD will hold me close (Psalm 27:10 NLT).

🕐 **Praying the Word**
Heavenly Father, be a loving parent to the multitude of orphans on this planet.

🌸 **Prayer Prompt**
Comfort, fill, bless, and call out these children who have been forgotten by all but You. Reveal Your love and plans for their lives. May they realize their destinies in You.

☕ Prayer Focus _____

📖 Scripture Inspiration

_____

_____

🕐 Praying the Word

_____

_____

❀ Prayer Prompt

_____

_____

_____

☕ Prayer Focus _____

📖 Scripture Inspiration

_____

_____

🕐 Praying the Word

_____

_____

❀ Prayer Prompt

_____

_____

_____

Day 9

Self

📖 Scripture Inspiration

Do not be anxious about anything, but in everything by prayer and supplication with thanksgiving let your requests be made known to God (Philippians 4:6).

☉ Praying the Word

I submit all of my worries and concerns to You, Lord. Thank You that You hear me and will answer according to Your will and character.

✿ Prayer Prompt

Make me a woman of prayer. God, I know there is power in my simple words, expressed before Your throne. Instead of carrying the weight of my concerns on my own shoulders, remind me to let them roll off and leave them at Your nail-scarred feet. Chief among those concerns are my precious grandchildren. Remind me to carry them often into Your presence for Your supernatural touch on their lives.

Prayer Focus _____

Scripture Inspiration

_____

_____

_____

_____

Praying the Word

_____

_____

_____

_____

_____

Prayer Prompt

_____

_____

_____

_____

_____

_____

_____

_____

Day 9
Adult Children

☕ **Prayer Focus**—Identity

📖 **Scripture Inspiration**

I have redeemed you; I have called you by name, you are mine (Isaiah 43:1).

☉ **Praying the Word**

Lord, whisper each of my children's names into their hearts. May Your love reach deep into their lives to bring peace and an assurance that they are Yours.

🌸 **Prayer Prompt**

May each of my children be, first and foremost, a child of God. Anchor their identity in Your love and acceptance of them. Grant them a glimpse of how You feel about them, how wonderful You think they are, and the amazing things You are working in them and through them. Answer their questions with Your love.

🍵 Prayer Focus _____

📖 Scripture Inspiration

_____

_____

_____

_____

🕑 Praying the Word

_____

_____

_____

_____

_____

_____

🌸 Prayer Prompt

_____

_____

_____

_____

_____

_____

_____

_____

_____

_____

Day 9
Grandchildren

☕ **Prayer Focus**—Mentors

📖 Scripture Inspiration

We loved you so much that we were delighted to share with you not only the gospel of God but our lives as well, because you had become so dear to us (1 Thessalonians 2:8 NIV).

☉ Praying the Word

Lord, raise up godly men and women to love my grand-children and to model Jesus before them by the way they talk and the way they live their lives.

🌸 Prayer Prompt

Give my grandchildren godly role models, mentors, and heroes. Beginning in their childhood, through their teenage years, and even when they're adults, place men and women in their paths who will take a special interest in them and guide them through the seasons of growing up. Give these mentors wisdom to affect my grandchildren's lives at pivotal moments to keep them on course for You.

🍵 Prayer Focus _____

📖 Scripture Inspiration

_____

_____

_____

_____

🕙 Praying the Word

_____

_____

_____

_____

_____

🌸 Prayer Prompt

_____

_____

_____

_____

_____

_____

_____

_____

_____

Day 9
Grandchildren's Future

☕ **Prayer Focus**—Responsibilities

📖 Scripture Inspiration

When I was a child, I spoke like a child, I thought like a child, I reasoned like a child. When I became a man, I gave up childish ways (1 Corinthians 13:11).

☉ Praying the Word

Enable my grandchildren to grow up, leave childhood behind, and become responsible adults.

🌸 Prayer Prompt

I thank You in advance, Lord, for blessed childhood experiences and memories for my grandchildren. I pray that their heritage will be a healthy foundation on which to build a strong future as adults. Give them an excitement for leaving the nest and soaring into their destinies. Help them establish good habits and godly character traits now that will enable them to one day handle much responsibility with wisdom and humility.

Prayer Focus _____

Scripture Inspiration

_____

_____

_____

_____

Praying the Word

_____

_____

_____

_____

_____

Prayer Prompt

_____

_____

_____

_____

_____

_____

_____

_____

Day 9
Grandchildren's Character

☕ **Prayer Focus**—Joy

📖 **Scripture Inspiration**
Ask, and you will receive, that your joy may be full (John 16:24).

🕐 **Praying the Word**
Jesus, I'm asking You to fill my grandchildren's hearts with gladness.

🌸 **Prayer Prompt**
Even more than I do, You desire my grandchildren to live in joy. In every circumstance let them know contentment, trust, hope, and true, Christ-centered joy.

Children of the World

☕ **Prayer Focus**—Victims of Tragedy

📖 **Scripture Inspiration**
How precious is your steadfast love, O God! The children of mankind take refuge in the shadow of your wings (Psalm 36:7).

🕐 **Praying the Word**
God, swoop in with Your love and rescue children whose lives have been turned upside down by tragedy.

🌸 **Prayer Prompt**
In the middle of this desperate, scary time in their lives, send Your Holy Spirit to comfort, save, and give hope for the future.

Prayer Focus _____

Scripture Inspiration

_____

_____

Praying the Word

_____

_____

Prayer Prompt

_____

_____

_____

Prayer Focus _____

Scripture Inspiration

_____

_____

Praying the Word

_____

_____

Prayer Prompt

_____

_____

_____

Day 10

Self

☕ **Prayer Focus**—My Future

📖 **Scripture Inspiration**

I know the plans I have for you, declares the LORD, plans for wholeness and not for evil, to give you a future and a hope (Jeremiah 29:11).

🕙 **Praying the Word**

Thank You, Lord, that You have my future in Your good and loving hands. I'm excited about what You have in store for me.

❀ **Prayer Prompt**

Almighty God, help me to trust You for my future. Keep my mind focused on Your merciful, faithful, extravagant character. I know Your plans for me are better than I could ever hope for on my own. I'm thankful that my immediate and, even more importantly, my eternal future is safe with You. Allow me to enjoy my future with You and these sweet grandchildren with whom You've blessed me.

Prayer Focus _____

Scripture Inspiration

_____
_____
_____
_____

Praying the Word

_____
_____
_____
_____
_____
_____

Prayer Prompt

_____
_____
_____
_____
_____
_____
_____
_____
_____

Day 10
Adult Children

☕ **Prayer Focus**—Health

📖 **Scripture Inspiration**

I will restore health to you, and your wounds I will heal, declares the LORD (Jeremiah 30:17).

⊘ **Praying the Word**

Give my children good health, and be their healer.

🌸 **Prayer Prompt**

Jesus, thank You for Your promise of healing, wholeness, and health. I stand on Your Word and claim this truth for my children. Heal them physically, emotionally, mentally, and spiritually of any wounds from which they are suffering or have suffered. Grant them abundant life in every sense of the word.

Prayer Focus _____

Scripture Inspiration

_____

_____

_____

_____

Praying the Word

_____

_____

_____

_____

_____

_____

Prayer Prompt

_____

_____

_____

_____

_____

_____

_____

_____

Day 10

Grandchildren

☕ **Prayer Focus**—Peer Pressure

📖 Scripture Inspiration

Whoever walks with the wise becomes wise, but the companion of fools will suffer harm (Proverbs 13:20).

☉ Praying the Word

Wise Counselor, teach my grandchildren to choose their friends carefully and prayerfully so they will reap benefits rather than consequences.

🌸 Prayer Prompt

First, secure my grandchildren so firmly in their identity as children called by God that they listen to Your voice above all others. Then surround them with friends who will draw them closer to You, not away. Give my grandchildren courage to stand up—to go against the crowd rather than merely follow—and lead others to You.

☕ Prayer Focus _____

📖 Scripture Inspiration

_____

_____

_____

_____

🕐 Praying the Word

_____

_____

_____

_____

_____

_____

🌸 Prayer Prompt

_____

_____

_____

_____

_____

_____

_____

_____

_____

Day 10
Grandchildren's Future

☕ **Prayer Focus**—Recreation

📖 **Scripture Inspiration**

One hand full of rest is better than two fists full of labor and striving after wind (Ecclesiastes 4:6 NASB).

☉ **Praying the Word**

Father, enable my grandchildren to enjoy healthy rest and recreation from their work.

🌸 **Prayer Prompt**

I pray that when my grandchildren become busy adults, they will trust You enough to know when to slow down and enjoy life. I pray that they will not strive for power or money or be trapped in perfectionism. Give them wholesome outlets for fun and relaxation. Establish a healthy balance between work and play. Instill in them a respect for Your command of a weekly time of Sabbath rest in their homes.

Prayer Focus _____

Scripture Inspiration

_____

_____

_____

_____

Praying the Word

_____

_____

_____

_____

_____

_____

Prayer Prompt

_____

_____

_____

_____

_____

_____

_____

_____

_____

_____

Day 10

Grandchildren's Character

☕ **Prayer Focus**—Peace

📖 **Scripture Inspiration**
Seek peace and pursue it (1 Peter 3:11).

🕙 **Praying the Word**
Father, I pray that my grandchildren will be peace-seekers and peacemakers.

❀ **Prayer Prompt**
Teach my grandchildren to trust You so completely that their peace is unshakable. May they submit all cares to You and leave them in Your capable hands. Help them also to live in peace with, and bring peace to, those around them.

Children of the World

☕ **Prayer Focus**—Foster Children

📖 **Scripture Inspiration**
Whoever receives one such child in my name receives me, and whoever receives me, receives not me but him who sent me (Mark 9:37).

🕙 **Praying the Word**
Heavenly Father, raise up foster parents to serve You by caring for Your children.

❀ **Prayer Prompt**
Pour an abundance of love into foster parents' hearts to care for the children in their homes. Enable these children to receive Your gift of love.

Prayer Focus _____

Scripture Inspiration

_____

_____

Praying the Word

_____

_____

Prayer Prompt

_____

_____

_____

Prayer Focus _____

Scripture Inspiration

_____

_____

Praying the Word

_____

_____

Prayer Prompt

_____

_____

_____

Day 11

Self

📖 Scripture Inspiration

I have stored up your word in my heart, that I might not sin against you (Psalm 119:11).

☉ Praying the Word

Lord, write Your Word on my heart. May its power and truth keep me from evil.

✿ Prayer Prompt

Take me to greater depths in my Bible study. My desire is to know You more fully, and I understand that soaking up the Scriptures is just what I need to become more intimately acquainted with You. As I read passages I've read many times before, allow them to "jump off the page" with fresh revelation for my life. Enable me to memorize Your Word so I might always be ready to point my grandchildren to You and Your ways.

Prayer Focus _____

Scripture Inspiration

_____

_____

_____

_____

Praying the Word

_____

_____

_____

_____

_____

_____

Prayer Prompt

_____

_____

_____

_____

_____

_____

_____

_____

_____

Day 11

Adult Children

☕ **Prayer Focus**—Finances

📖 Scripture Inspiration

May the LORD give you increase, you and your children (Psalm 115:14).

☉ Praying the Word

Lord, You have already given my children and me so much; now I'm asking You to multiply those gifts exponentially.

❀ Prayer Prompt

Thank You that Your heart's desire is to give abundantly and extravagantly to Your children (which also happen to be my children). It's amazing to me that You don't consider it selfish or greedy when we pray for more. We're simply asking in line with Your character, Your will, and Your love for us: pour out Your blessings on my children and their children.

Prayer Focus _____

Scripture Inspiration

_____

_____

_____

_____

Praying the Word

_____

_____

_____

_____

_____

Prayer Prompt

_____

_____

_____

_____

_____

_____

_____

_____

Day 11

Grandchildren

☕ **Prayer Focus**—Stranger Danger

📖 Scripture Inspiration

Wisdom will save you from the ways of wicked men, from men whose words are perverse (Proverbs 2:12 NIV).

☉ Praying the Word

Father, deposit in my grandchildren's hearts a measure of discernment that will protect them from evil. May they follow Your voice, and not that of a stranger.

✿ Prayer Prompt

Oh, Lord, keep my grandchildren safe. Assign your biggest, baddest, burliest angels to surround them on every side. Thwart any plan of the enemy to harm them. Encourage my grandchildren to listen to that still, small voice of warning and caution if ever in the presence of danger or evil. Give them wisdom to know what to do in any threatening situation. Better yet, just keep them out of trouble of any kind.

Prayer Focus _____

Scripture Inspiration

_____

_____

_____

_____

Praying the Word

_____

_____

_____

_____

_____

_____

Prayer Prompt

_____

_____

_____

_____

_____

_____

_____

_____

Day 11
Grandchildren's Future

☕ **Prayer Focus**—Service

📖 **Scripture Inspiration**

Even the Son of Man came not to be served but to serve, and to give his life as a ransom for many (Mark 10:45).

☉ **Praying the Word**

Jesus, may my grandchildren grow up to follow in Your footsteps of sacrificial service to others.

🌸 **Prayer Prompt**

I pray that my grandchildren will come to know the deep satisfaction that results from giving their lives away. Once they've tasted the joy of serving others, may that joy and service characterize their lives forever. Encourage them to seek opportunities to give of themselves out of the abundance You've given to them.

Prayer Focus _____

Scripture Inspiration

_____

_____

_____

_____

Praying the Word

_____

_____

_____

_____

_____

_____

Prayer Prompt

_____

_____

_____

_____

_____

_____

_____

_____

_____

Day 11

Grandchildren's Character

☕ **Prayer Focus**—Patience

📖 **Scripture Inspiration**
The Lord's servant must not be quarrelsome but kind to everyone, able to teach, patiently enduring evil (2 Timothy 2:24).

🕙 **Praying the Word**
Lord, place in my grandchildren's hearts Spirit-empowered patience, enabling them to speak wise words of peace and reconciliation.

🌸 **Prayer Prompt**
Patience is definitely a gift. So I'm asking Your Spirit to be present in my grandchildren in such a way that they display supernatural patience, even as little children.

Children of the World

☕ **Prayer Focus**—Physically Abused

📖 **Scripture Inspiration**
He sent out his word and healed them, and delivered them from their destruction (Psalm 107:20).

🕙 **Praying the Word**
Almighty God, heal and deliver children who are abused.

🌸 **Prayer Prompt**
Expose any physical abuse that's going on, and bring these children into the light, where they can be cared for and protected. Be their defender and healer.

☕ Prayer Focus _____

📖 Scripture Inspiration

_____

_____

🕓 Praying the Word

_____

_____

❀ Prayer Prompt

_____

_____

_____

☕ Prayer Focus _____

📖 Scripture Inspiration

_____

_____

🕓 Praying the Word

_____

_____

❀ Prayer Prompt

_____

_____

_____

Day 12

Self

☕ **Prayer Focus**—Finances

📖 **Scripture Inspiration**

Do not fear; I will provide for you and your little ones (Genesis 50:21).

🕗 **Praying the Word**

I am grateful, Lord, for Your provision. Thank You for understanding my anxieties about money and my desire to buy things for my grandchildren. I will trust You to take care of me and these precious little ones.

🌸 **Prayer Prompt**

Heavenly Father, I know that You will supply all of my needs. Would you also provide some of my wants, especially the things I want to share with my grandchildren? I will rest in Your ability to bless my todays and secure my tomorrows. Teach me how to be a good steward of the finances You've provided, and help me find the right balance between saving for the future and living openhandedly.

🍵 Prayer Focus _____

📖 Scripture Inspiration

_____
_____
_____
_____

🕐 Praying the Word

_____
_____
_____
_____
_____
_____

🌸 Prayer Prompt

_____
_____
_____
_____
_____
_____
_____
_____
_____

Day 12
Adult Children

☕ **Prayer Focus**—Walking with God

📖 **Scripture Inspiration**

I have no greater joy than to hear that my children are walking in the truth (3 John 4).

🕐 **Praying the Word**

Father, allow me the joy of seeing my children follow You with all their hearts.

🌸 **Prayer Prompt**

Draw my children into a deeper relationship with You, Lord. Meet them in a personal way during their times of prayer. Speak to them through Your Word. Surround them with Your presence during worship. Open their ears to hear You, their eyes to see Your will, and their hearts to receive Your friendship.

☕ Prayer Focus _____

📖 Scripture Inspiration

_____
_____
_____
_____

☉ Praying the Word

_____
_____
_____
_____
_____
_____

❀ Prayer Prompt

_____
_____
_____
_____
_____
_____
_____
_____
_____
_____

Day 12
Grandchildren

☕ **Prayer Focus**—Identity

📖 **Scripture Inspiration**

For this reason I bow my knees before the Father, . . . that you, being rooted and grounded in love, may have strength to comprehend with all the saints what is the breadth and length and height and depth, and to know the love of Christ that surpasses knowledge (Ephesians 3:14, 17–19).

☉ **Praying the Word**

Father, may my grandchildren be assured of Your love in the very depths of their being.

🌸 **Prayer Prompt**

I pray that my grandchildren will never question Your love for them. Teach them that Your love is not a feeling; it is a fact. May they always, and only, look to You to discover who they are and why they were created. Teach them to trust You enough to submit their lives to You and truly make You Lord.

Prayer Focus _____

Scripture Inspiration

_____

_____

_____

_____

Praying the Word

_____

_____

_____

_____

_____

Prayer Prompt

_____

_____

_____

_____

_____

_____

_____

_____

_____

Day 12
Grandchildren's Future

☕ **Prayer Focus**—Marriage

📖Scripture Inspiration

Let each one of you love his wife as himself, and let the wife see that she respects her husband (Ephesians 5:33).

☉ Praying the Word

I pray for a healthy, loving marriage for each of my grandchildren—one in which each spouse serves the other.

🌸 Prayer Prompt

Give my grandchildren healthy, solid marriages that model Your love for the church. Enable the husbands to love their wives sacrificially and the wives to express admiration liberally. Grant that each of my grandchildren will know the sweet gift of a happy, Christ-centered marriage.

Prayer Focus _____

Scripture Inspiration

_____

_____

_____

_____

Praying the Word

_____

_____

_____

_____

_____

Prayer Prompt

_____

_____

_____

_____

_____

_____

_____

_____

Day 12
Grandchildren's Character

☕ **Prayer Focus**—Kindness

📖 **Scripture Inspiration**
What does the Lord require of you but to do justice, and to love kindness, and to walk humbly with your God (Micah 6:8).

🕒 **Praying the Word**
God, may my grandchildren walk in humility, fairness, and kindness before You all the days of their lives.

🌼 **Prayer Prompt**
Make my grandchildren's hearts tender so their words and actions will be saturated with kindness. Show them how to extend kindness to a hurting world.

Children of the World

☕ **Prayer Focus**—Emotionally Abused

📖 **Scripture Inspiration**
He heals the brokenhearted and binds up their wounds (Psalm 147:3).

🕒 **Praying the Word**
Thank You, Lord, that You see the broken hearts and tears cried in the night.

🌼 **Prayer Prompt**
Jesus, You came to heal the brokenhearted. Wrap Your loving arms around the hurting children today, and heal them with a touch of Your nail-scarred hands.

🍵 Prayer Focus _____

📖 Scripture Inspiration

_____

_____

🕐 Praying the Word

_____

_____

🌸 Prayer Prompt

_____

_____

_____

🍵 Prayer Focus _____

📖 Scripture Inspiration

_____

_____

🕐 Praying the Word

_____

_____

🌸 Prayer Prompt

_____

_____

_____

Day 13

Self

☕ **Prayer Focus**—Worship

📖 **Scripture Inspiration**

The hour is coming, and is now here, when the true worshipers will worship the Father in spirit and truth (John 4:23).

☉ **Praying the Word**

I want to be a true worshiper. Father, fill me today with Your Spirit and truth, that I might turn around and offer my adoration back to You.

❀ **Prayer Prompt**

I love You, Lord, and I lift up Your holy name in adoration. May my offering of praise be a sweet aroma before Your throne. Open my eyes to see You in all your glory so that worship will flow through my lips from my heart. I pray that my worship will be as natural as breathing. Allow my grandchildren to catch a glimpse of You as I extol Your greatness.

Prayer Focus _____

Scripture Inspiration

_____
_____
_____
_____

Praying the Word

_____
_____
_____
_____
_____
_____

Prayer Prompt

_____
_____
_____
_____
_____
_____
_____
_____
_____
_____

Day 13
Adult Children

☕ **Prayer Focus**—Goals

📖 **Scripture Inspiration**

The heart of man plans his way, but the LORD establishes his steps (Proverbs 16:9).

☉ **Praying the Word**

King of heaven, reign in my children's hearts so that their goals are in line with Your will.

🌸 **Prayer Prompt**

Give my children a deep sense of calling and a keen awareness of Your purposes for their lives. Allow them to see where You're working so they can partner with You as You write their life stories. Speak promises to their hearts, and give them faith to believe You will bring those things to pass. May the goals they set for their lives be initiated by Your Spirit. Enable them to envision with hope and faith those plans coming to fruition even when they are yet seeds of promise.

Prayer Focus _____

Scripture Inspiration

_____

_____

_____

_____

Praying the Word

_____

_____

_____

_____

_____

Prayer Prompt

_____

_____

_____

_____

_____

_____

_____

_____

Day 13
Grandchildren

Prayer Focus—Relationship with Parents

Scripture Inspiration

Honor your father and your mother, that your days may be long in the land that the LORD your God is giving you (Exodus 20:12).

Praying the Word

I pray that my grandchildren would submit to their parents and trust their wisdom to lead them to safety and success.

Prayer Prompt

Heavenly Father, place in my grandchildren's hearts a reverent fear in light of their parents' position of authority. From that foundation of healthy respect, knit together the hearts of each parent and child with mercy and grace. I pray that they will see their father and mother as their heroes, teachers, and closest friends.

Prayer Focus _____

Scripture Inspiration

_____
_____
_____
_____

Praying the Word

_____
_____
_____
_____
_____
_____

Prayer Prompt

_____
_____
_____
_____
_____
_____
_____
_____
_____

Day 13
Grandchildren's Future

☕ **Prayer Focus**—Acceptance of Self

📖 Scripture Inspiration

I praise you, for I am fearfully and wonderfully made. Wonderful are your works; my soul knows it very well (Psalm 139:14).

☉ Praying the Word

Wonderful Creator, help my grandchildren to love and accept themselves just the way You've made them.

✿ Prayer Prompt

I pray that my grandchildren will never desire to be anyone other than whom You've created them to be. Keep them from coveting the gifts, talents, or possessions of anyone else. While keeping in them a right sense of humility, give them also a deep sense of security that they are extraordinary and highly valuable in Your sight.

Prayer Focus _____

Scripture Inspiration

_____

_____

_____

_____

Praying the Word

_____

_____

_____

_____

_____

_____

Prayer Prompt

_____

_____

_____

_____

_____

_____

_____

_____

_____

Day 13
Grandchildren's Character

☕ **Prayer Focus**—Gentleness

📖 **Scripture Inspiration**

If anyone is caught in any transgression, you who are spiritual should restore him in a spirit of gentleness. Keep watch on yourself, lest you too be tempted (Galatians 6:1).

🕘 **Praying the Word**

Let my grandchildren be characterized by gentleness.

🌸 **Prayer Prompt**

Smooth the rough edges, and soften their words with the oil of Your Spirit. Show my grandchildren how to handle others with tender, loving care.

Children of the World

☕ **Prayer Focus**—Different Religions

📖 **Scripture Inspiration**

The LORD is . . . not willing that any should perish but that all should come to repentance (2 Peter 3:9 NKJV).

🕘 **Praying the Word**

Lord, I pray in accordance with Your will that all of Your children will know life and forgiveness in You.

🌸 **Prayer Prompt**

God, I lift up every child who is being raised in a religion that worships any but You. Open their eyes, whisper truth to them by Your Spirit, and draw them to Your Son.

☕ Prayer Focus _____

📖 Scripture Inspiration

_____
_____

⏱ Praying the Word

_____
_____

❀ Prayer Prompt

_____
_____
_____

☕ Prayer Focus _____

📖 Scripture Inspiration

_____
_____

⏱ Praying the Word

_____
_____

❀ Prayer Prompt

_____
_____
_____

Day 14

Self

📖 Scripture Inspiration

I have counsel and sound wisdom; I have insight; I have strength (Proverbs 8:14).

☉ Praying the Word

God, give me insight and strength that I may counsel with Your wisdom.

❀ Prayer Prompt

I want to see things through Your eyes of wisdom and love. Remind me to look at every relationship and every situation from Your perspective, not my own. Enable me to see the heart of the matter—and the person—with supernatural vision that comes from You. Give me keen perception and intuition from Your Spirit into the lives of my grandchildren so I can offer words of truth to them.

Prayer Focus _____

📖 Scripture Inspiration

_____

_____

_____

_____

🌙 Praying the Word

_____

_____

_____

_____

_____

🌸 Prayer Prompt

_____

_____

_____

_____

_____

_____

_____

_____

_____

Day 14
Adult Children

☕ **Prayer Focus**—Ministry

📖 **Scripture Inspiration**

I do not account my life of any value nor as precious to myself, if only I may finish my course and the ministry that I received from the Lord Jesus, to testify to the gospel of the grace of God (Acts 20:24).

🕑 **Praying the Word**

More than in any other area, I pray for my children's success in Your eyes, Lord. May they fulfill the purposes for which You have created them and be witnesses of Your grace.

🌼 **Prayer Prompt**

I have known my children are extraordinary from the first moment I laid eyes on them. Seal in their hearts a sense of destiny. Speak to them of the unique ministry for which You've created them. Encourage them to step out in Your strength to serve others and to proclaim the good news of life in You.

Prayer Focus _____

Scripture Inspiration

_____

_____

_____

_____

Praying the Word

_____

_____

_____

_____

_____

Prayer Prompt

_____

_____

_____

_____

_____

_____

_____

_____

Day 14
Grandchildren

☕ **Prayer Focus**—Relationship with Siblings

📖 Scripture Inspiration

Concerning brotherly love you have no need for anyone to write to you, for you yourselves have been taught by God to love one another (1 Thessalonians 4:9).

☉ Praying the Word

Lord, teach my grandchildren how to love their siblings with supernatural love that comes from You.

🌸 Prayer Prompt

I boldly pray that my grandchildren would consider their siblings their best friends. Dissolve any unhealthy competition or rivalry. Keep them close all the days of their lives. Help them to understand that they're on the same team and to cheer each other on, together against the world—or more appropriately, together *for* the world and the people You love who are in it.

Prayer Focus _____

Scripture Inspiration

_____
_____
_____
_____

Praying the Word

_____
_____
_____
_____
_____

Prayer Prompt

_____
_____
_____
_____
_____
_____
_____
_____

Day 14
Grandchildren's Future

☕ **Prayer Focus**—Leadership

📖 Scripture Inspiration

The Lord said to me, "Do not say, 'I am only a youth'; for to all to whom I send you, you shall go, and whatever I command you, you shall speak" (Jeremiah 1:7).

☉ Praying the Word

Lord, anoint my grandchildren from an early age to be leaders, and give them the courage to say and do whatever You command.

❀ Prayer Prompt

I believe my grandchildren will make a difference to many others around them. Whether they become obvious leaders or gentle influencers, I know You have plans to use them for Your kingdom. Help them to accept this responsibility with sobriety and strength of character.

Prayer Focus _____

Scripture Inspiration

_____
_____
_____
_____

Praying the Word

_____
_____
_____
_____
_____

Prayer Prompt

_____
_____
_____
_____
_____
_____
_____
_____

Day 14

Grandchildren's Character

☕ **Prayer Focus**—Self-Control

📖 **Scripture Inspiration**

A man without self-control is like a city broken into and left without walls (Proverbs 25:28).

🕐 **Praying the Word**

Father, build up my grandchildren's self-control so they might be protected—from the inside out.

🌸 **Prayer Prompt**

Strengthen my grandchildren: enable them to deny their flesh and choose Your Spirit. Teach them to respond righteously, live moderately, and triumph victoriously.

Children of the World

☕ **Prayer Focus**—Victims of Predators

📖 **Scripture Inspiration**

Rescue the weak and the needy; deliver them from the hand of the wicked (Psalm 82:4).

🕐 **Praying the Word**

God, protect children under threat from people with wicked intentions.

🌸 **Prayer Prompt**

Whether these children are victimized through the Internet, abduction, incest, molestation, or any other predatory evil, rescue Your little ones.

🍵 Prayer Focus _____

📖 Scripture Inspiration

_____

_____

🕙 Praying the Word

_____

_____

🌸 Prayer Prompt

_____

_____

_____

🍵 Prayer Focus _____

📖 Scripture Inspiration

_____

_____

🕙 Praying the Word

_____

_____

🌸 Prayer Prompt

_____

_____

_____

Day 15

Self

📖 Scripture Inspiration

Whatever your hand finds to do, do it with your might (Ecclesiastes 9:10).

☉ Praying the Word

Thank You, God, for the work You have given me to do. Strengthen me to do the best job I can.

🌸 Prayer Prompt

Lord, I'm grateful that You've given me meaningful work to accomplish. Even in the midst of the mundane, You make my tasks worthwhile because I can offer them as a holy sacrifice to You. Remind me that, ultimately, I am serving You in everything I say or do. Enable me to pass on a good work ethic, respect for authority, diligence in service, and a joyful attitude to my always-watching, ever-listening grandchildren.

☕ Prayer Focus _____

📖 Scripture Inspiration

_____
_____
_____
_____

◎ Praying the Word

_____
_____
_____
_____
_____

🌸 Prayer Prompt

_____
_____
_____
_____
_____
_____
_____
_____

Day 15
Adult Children

☕ **Prayer Focus**—Temptation

📖 **Scripture Inspiration**

God is faithful, and he will not let you be tempted beyond your ability, but with the temptation he will also provide the way of escape, that you may be able to endure it (1 Corinthians 10:13).

🕉 **Praying the Word**

Thank You, Lord, for providing for my children a way of escape from any and all temptations they may encounter.

🌼 **Prayer Prompt**

Keep my children walking close to You. If they are drawn away, pull them back close to Your side. Open their eyes to see the way of escape You have prepared for them, and give them the strength to resist temptation's tug. Bring all lies from the enemy into Your light so my children may see the truth—and give them the power to choose accordingly.

🍵 Prayer Focus _____

📖 Scripture Inspiration

_____
_____
_____
_____

🕐 Praying the Word

_____
_____
_____
_____
_____

🌸 Prayer Prompt

_____
_____
_____
_____
_____
_____
_____
_____

Day 15
Grandchildren

☕ **Prayer Focus**—Love the Word

📖 Scripture Inspiration

From childhood you have been acquainted with the sacred writings, which are able to make you wise for salvation through faith in Christ Jesus (2 Timothy 3:15).

☉ Praying the Word

Jesus, write Your Word on my grandchildren's hearts, and give them faith to believe that You are the way, the truth, and the life.

🌸 Prayer Prompt

Make my grandchildren hungry for Your Word. Give them a taste for truth from an early age. Help them to understand what You're saying to them, and direct them to seek You—and find you—in the Scriptures. Establish in them a habit of reading their Bibles every day to find the answers for life.

🍵 Prayer Focus _____

📖 Scripture Inspiration

_____
_____
_____
_____

🕘 Praying the Word

_____
_____
_____
_____
_____

🌸 Prayer Prompt

_____
_____
_____
_____
_____
_____
_____
_____
_____

Day 15
Grandchildren's Future

☕ **Prayer Focus**—Time Management

📖 Scripture Inspiration

For everything there is a season, and a time for every matter under heaven (Ecclesiastes 3:1).

☾ Praying the Word

Lord, give my grandchildren wisdom to discern the right time and place for everything.

🌸 Prayer Prompt

Thank You for the precious gift of time—a gift You've given to each of us. I pray that my grandchildren will learn to steward it wisely. As they go through life, show them Your perspective on what is important and worthy. Help them develop a healthy balance in their lives. Above all, may they spend time seeking You—and from that investment let everything else fall into place.

🍵 Prayer Focus _____

📖 Scripture Inspiration

_____

_____

_____

_____

🕙 Praying the Word

_____

_____

_____

_____

_____

_____

🌼 Prayer Prompt

_____

_____

_____

_____

_____

_____

_____

_____

_____

Day 15

Grandchildren's Character

☕ **Prayer Focus**—Wisdom

📖 **Scripture Inspiration**

The child grew and became strong, filled with wisdom. And the favor of God was upon him (Luke 2:40).

🕐 **Praying the Word**

God, grant my grandchildren favor, and fill them with Your wisdom.

❀ **Prayer Prompt**

Guide them. Enable them to understand situations as You do and to know how to respond. Help them to share Your wisdom through prudent speech and actions.

Children of the World

☕ **Prayer Focus**—Financial Help

📖 **Scripture Inspiration**

If anyone has the world's goods and sees his brother in need, yet closes his heart against him, how does God's love abide in him? (1 John 3:17).

🕐 **Praying the Word**

God, move people's hearts to give generously to children who are less fortunate.

❀ **Prayer Prompt**

Encourage Your adult children to show tangible evidence of Your love by giving to needy children around the world.

☕ **Prayer Focus** _____

📖 Scripture Inspiration

_____
_____

🕙 Praying the Word

_____
_____

❀ Prayer Prompt

_____
_____
_____

☕ **Prayer Focus** _____

📖 Scripture Inspiration

_____
_____

🕙 Praying the Word

_____
_____

❀ Prayer Prompt

_____
_____
_____

151

Day 16

Self

📖 Scripture Inspiration

Your body is a temple of the Holy Spirit within you (1 Corinthians 6:19).

⊙ Praying the Word

Thank You, Holy Spirit, for the privilege of being Your dwelling place. Keep me strong and healthy for Your service.

🌸 Prayer Prompt

Lord, help me to love my body and to accept it, if only because You have made it Your home. I want to eat healthily and get regular exercise so I can serve You with strength and vigor for many more years. Help me to be more disciplined in these areas so I can enjoy pain-free play with my grandchildren and abundant life in You.

☕ Prayer Focus _____

📖 Scripture Inspiration

_____

_____

_____

_____

⑤ Praying the Word

_____

_____

_____

_____

_____

_____

🌸 Prayer Prompt

_____

_____

_____

_____

_____

_____

_____

_____

153

Day 16

Adult Children

☕ **Prayer Focus**—Forgiveness

📖 Scripture Inspiration

If you forgive others their trespasses, your heavenly Father will also forgive you (Matthew 6:14).

☉ Praying the Word

Father, let my children demonstrate Your forgiveness—of themselves and of others.

🌸 Prayer Prompt

Allow Your forgiveness to flow freely to and through my children. Enable them to fully accept Your forgiveness of their sins, understanding that You choose not even to remember them. To the degree they have received Your gift of mercy, let them extend it to any who hurt them or in some way sin against them.

🍵 Prayer Focus _____

📖 Scripture Inspiration

_____
_____
_____
_____

☉ Praying the Word

_____
_____
_____
_____
_____
_____

🌸 Prayer Prompt

_____
_____
_____
_____
_____
_____
_____
_____
_____

Day 16
Grandchildren

☕ **Prayer Focus**—Internet

📖 Scripture Inspiration

Flee youthful passions and pursue righteousness, faith, love, and peace, along with those who call on the Lord from a pure heart (2 Timothy 2:22).

☉ Praying the Word

Lord, teach my grandchildren to chase hard after You and to run from anything that is not pleasing in Your sight. Show them the importance of surrounding themselves with pure influences.

🌸 Prayer Prompt

I thank You for the Internet, but I also know it can be a two-edged sword. Protect my grandchildren from dangers lurking on the World Wide Web. Strengthen them to resist temptation to visit sites they shouldn't visit. Give their parents wisdom to know how to take advantage of the good without making their children vulnerable to the bad.

☕ Prayer Focus _____

📖 Scripture Inspiration

_____
_____
_____
_____

🕒 Praying the Word

_____
_____
_____
_____
_____
_____

🌸 Prayer Prompt

_____
_____
_____
_____
_____
_____
_____
_____

Day 16
Grandchildren's Future

☕ **Prayer Focus**—Parenting

📖 Scripture Inspiration

These words that I command you today shall be on your heart. You shall teach them diligently to your children, and shall talk of them when you sit in your house, and when you walk by the way, and when you lie down, and when you rise (Deuteronomy 6:6–7).

☉ Praying the Word

God, anoint my grandchildren to teach their children Your ways.

🌸 Prayer Prompt

Equip my grandchildren for the awesome task and responsibility of raising the next generation of believers. Fill their hearts with a love for Your Word and the power to live it out before their families. May Your truths flow naturally from their lips and their lives. Give them wisdom to raise godly children who love and fear You.

Prayer Focus _____

Scripture Inspiration

_____

_____

_____

_____

Praying the Word

_____

_____

_____

_____

_____

Prayer Prompt

_____

_____

_____

_____

_____

_____

_____

_____

Day 16

Grandchildren's Character

☕ **Prayer Focus**—Sharing

📖 **Scripture Inspiration**

Do not neglect to do good and to share what you have, for such sacrifices are pleasing to God (Hebrews 13:16).

🕐 **Praying the Word**

Father, teach my grandchildren to share, and let them feel Your pleasure when they do.

❀ **Prayer Prompt**

Enable my grandchildren to live openhandedly, understanding that clenched hands are unable to receive from You but that sharing with others enables them to share in Your bounty.

Children of the World

☕ **Prayer Focus**—Salvation

📖 **Scripture Inspiration**

Jesus said to him, "I am the way, and the truth, and the life. No one comes to the Father except through me" (John 14:6).

🕐 **Praying the Word**

Lord, have mercy on the children of the world, and save them.

❀ **Prayer Prompt**

Send Your Word to the ends of the earth, proclaiming the Good News of Jesus Christ. Prepare the hearts of children everywhere to receive You as Lord.

☕ Prayer Focus _____

📖 Scripture Inspiration

_____

_____

🕘 Praying the Word

_____

_____

🌸 Prayer Prompt

_____

_____

_____

☕ Prayer Focus _____

📖 Scripture Inspiration

_____

_____

🕘 Praying the Word

_____

_____

🌸 Prayer Prompt

_____

_____

_____

Day 17

Self

☕ **Prayer Focus**—Thoughts

📖 Scripture Inspiration

Whatever is true, whatever is honorable, whatever is just, whatever is pure, whatever is lovely, whatever is commendable, if there is any excellence, if there is anything worthy of praise, think about these things (Philippians 4:8).

☉ Praying the Word

Father, gird up my mind so that I only think thoughts that are pleasing to You.

❀ Prayer Prompt

I know that my thoughts are important. They affect my words, my actions, my habits, and my character. Whenever negative thoughts, lies from the enemy, unworthy ruminations, or worldly influences creep into (or out of) the recesses of my mind, enable me to take those thoughts captive to the obedience of Christ. Deal with the root of the problem so my thoughts will be pleasing to You.

Prayer Focus _____

Scripture Inspiration

_____

_____

_____

_____

Praying the Word

_____

_____

_____

_____

_____

_____

Prayer Prompt

_____

_____

_____

_____

_____

_____

_____

_____

Day 17
Adult Children

☕ **Prayer Focus**—Past Experiences

📖 **Scripture Inspiration**

Remember not the former things, nor consider the things of old. Behold, I am doing a new thing; now it springs forth, do you not perceive it? I will make a way in the wilderness and rivers in the desert (Isaiah 43:18–19).

⟳ **Praying the Word**

God, help my children to forget the past and to see the new work You're doing in them and for them.

✿ **Prayer Prompt**

Thank You for the things You're doing in my children's lives. Open their eyes to see what You are creating, even out of the pain of the past. Wash over their past hurts and failures with Your cleansing blood. Allow them to see their future the way You see it—bright with promise and hope.

Prayer Focus _____

Scripture Inspiration

_____

_____

_____

_____

Praying the Word

_____

_____

_____

_____

_____

Prayer Prompt

_____

_____

_____

_____

_____

_____

_____

_____

_____

Day 17
Grandchildren

☕ **Prayer Focus**—Music

📖Scripture Inspiration

It is better for a man to hear the rebuke of the wise than to hear the song of fools (Ecclesiastes 7:5).

☉ Praying the Word

Teach my grandchildren to listen to wisdom and reject foolishness.

🌸 Prayer Prompt

Thank You, God, for the gift of music. May it always draw my grandchildren closer to You rather than to the world. Show them the importance of being careful what they allow through their ears and into their hearts. Make their spirits so sensitive that any music that doesn't glorify You and what you consider worthy would be like an irritating noise to their souls.

Prayer Focus _____

Scripture Inspiration

_____

_____

_____

_____

Praying the Word

_____

_____

_____

_____

_____

Prayer Prompt

_____

_____

_____

_____

_____

_____

_____

_____

_____

Day 17
Grandchildren's Future

☕ **Prayer Focus**—Walking with God

📖Scripture Inspiration

Abide in me, and I in you. As the branch cannot bear fruit by itself, unless it abides in the vine, neither can you unless you abide in me (John 15:4).

☉ Praying the Word

Jesus, make my grandchildren's number one goal in life to have a deep, abiding relationship with You.

🌸Prayer Prompt

My heart cries out on behalf of my grandchildren: all the days of their lives, draw them into a personal relationship with You, Lord. Open their ears to hear Your voice; give them faith to trust and obey You; fill their hearts until they overflow with worship. Give them a hunger for Your Word. Mold them into men and women of powerful prayer. And may they always rest in Your love.

Prayer Focus _____

Scripture Inspiration

_____

_____

_____

_____

Praying the Word

_____

_____

_____

_____

_____

Prayer Prompt

_____

_____

_____

_____

_____

_____

_____

_____

_____

Day 17

Grandchildren's Character

☕ **Prayer Focus**—Forgiveness

📖 **Scripture Inspiration**

Be kind to one another, tenderhearted, forgiving one another, as God in Christ forgave you (Ephesians 4:32).

🕐 **Praying the Word**

Create in my grandchildren sensitive, merciful hearts that are quick to forgive.

🌸 **Prayer Prompt**

I pray that receiving and extending forgiveness will become as natural for them as breathing. Keep the flow of mercy and grace unobstructed in my grandchildren's lives.

Children of the World

☕ **Prayer Focus**—Big Brothers and Big Sisters

📖 **Scripture Inspiration**

We dealt with each of you as a father deals with his own children, encouraging, comforting and urging you to live lives worthy of God (1 Thessalonians 2:11–12 NIV).

🕐 **Praying the Word**

Lord, encourage believers to take children under their wings and lead them to abundant life in You.

🌸 **Prayer Prompt**

God, it seems You should have enough followers to assign one to every lonely child. Raise up an army of "big brothers" and "big sisters."

☕ **Prayer Focus** _____

📖 Scripture Inspiration

_____

_____

🕙 Praying the Word

_____

_____

❀ Prayer Prompt

_____

_____

_____

☕ **Prayer Focus** _____

📖 Scripture Inspiration

_____

_____

🕙 Praying the Word

_____

_____

❀ Prayer Prompt

_____

_____

_____

Day 18

Self

📖 Scripture Inspiration

We impart this in words not taught by human wisdom but taught by the Spirit, interpreting spiritual truths to those who are spiritual (1 Corinthians 2:13).

☉ Praying the Word

I don't want to give advice; I want to offer supernatural wisdom from above. Fill me with Your Spirit, Lord, and let my words spring from that abundance.

🌸 Prayer Prompt

I want to speak words of life to my grandchildren. I begin by asking You to give me a liberal dose of wisdom. Hide Your Word in my heart in such a familiar way that my words reflect Your own. Give me opportunities to impart Your seeds of truth in such practical and winsome ways that their hearts soak them up and bear fruit for years to come.

Prayer Focus _____

Scripture Inspiration

_____

_____

_____

_____

Praying the Word

_____

_____

_____

_____

_____

_____

Prayer Prompt

_____

_____

_____

_____

_____

_____

_____

_____

_____

Day 18
Adult Children

☕ **Prayer Focus**—Retirement Years

📖 Scripture Inspiration

They still bear fruit in old age; they are ever full of sap and green (Psalm 92:14).

☉ Praying the Word

Ageless Lord, give my children productive days all the days of their lives. May they never stop growing.

🌸 Prayer Prompt

I probably won't be around for my children's golden years, but You will. So I'm asking You now to bless them. Give them health, abundance, joy, purpose, peace, and meaningful ministry. Anoint my grandchildren to lovingly care for my children, even as they have been sacrificially loved.

🍵 Prayer Focus _____

📖 Scripture Inspiration

_____

_____

_____

_____

🕐 Praying the Word

_____

_____

_____

_____

_____

_____

🌸 Prayer Prompt

_____

_____

_____

_____

_____

_____

_____

_____

_____

_____

Day 18

Grandchildren

Prayer Focus—Movies and Television

Scripture Inspiration

Do not love the world or the things in the world. If anyone loves the world, the love of the Father is not in him (1 John 2:15).

☉ Praying the Word

Father, fill my grandchildren with Your love with such intensity that nothing the world has to offer can draw them away from You.

Prayer Prompt

Give my grandchildren wisdom, discernment, sensitivity, and self-control when it comes to their media choices. May their souls be so pure that the evil that's on television and in movies would not even be attractive to them. As they grow older, teach them to make healthy viewing choices out of respect for You and a desire for untainted fellowship with the Holy Spirit.

Prayer Focus _____

Scripture Inspiration

_____

_____

_____

_____

Praying the Word

_____

_____

_____

_____

_____

Prayer Prompt

_____

_____

_____

_____

_____

_____

_____

_____

Day 18
Grandchildren's Future

☕ **Prayer Focus**—Protection from the Enemy

📖 Scripture Inspiration

The LORD is faithful. He will establish you and guard you against the evil one (2 Thessalonians 3:3).

☉ Praying the Word

Thank You, God, that You have already promised to defend Your plans for my grandchildren.

❀ Prayer Prompt

Lord, I know You have great plans for my grandchildren. I also know the enemy would love to come in and rob, kill, and destroy. I am standing in the gap for my grandchildren, asking You to commission warring angels in the heavenlies to thwart the plans of the enemy. Safeguard these who are precious to You (and to me).

Prayer Focus _____

Scripture Inspiration

_____
_____
_____
_____

Praying the Word

_____
_____
_____
_____
_____
_____

Prayer Prompt

_____
_____
_____
_____
_____
_____
_____
_____
_____
_____

Day 18

Grandchildren's Character

☕ **Prayer Focus**—Respect for Authority

📖 **Scripture Inspiration**
There is no authority except from God, and those that exist have been instituted by God (Romans 13:1).

🕐 **Praying the Word**
Lord, teach my grandchildren a healthy respect for authority.

🌸 **Prayer Prompt**
Reveal Your awesomeness so they will regard You with reverent fear. Out of that respect, teach them to also respect other authority figures. Show them the ultimate freedom in obedience.

Children of the World

☕ **Prayer Focus**—Prodigal Children

📖 **Scripture Inspiration**
There is hope for your future, declares the LORD, and your children shall come back to their own country (Jeremiah 31:17).

🕐 **Praying the Word**
Lord, give hope to heartbroken parents that You will rescue their straying children.

🌸 **Prayer Prompt**
Open every prodigal child's eyes to see the futility of life without You. Bring them home safely to forgiveness and an eternal embrace.

☕ Prayer Focus _____

📖 Scripture Inspiration

_____

_____

🕙 Praying the Word

_____

_____

🌸 Prayer Prompt

_____

_____

_____

☕ Prayer Focus _____

📖 Scripture Inspiration

_____

_____

🕙 Praying the Word

_____

_____

🌸 Prayer Prompt

_____

_____

_____

Day 19

Self

📖 **Scripture Inspiration**

Even to your old age I am he, and to gray hairs I will carry you. I have made, and I will bear; I will carry and will save (Isaiah 46:4).

⊙ **Praying the Word**

Lord, I will rest in You and trust You to take care of me all the days of my life.

✿ **Prayer Prompt**

Dear God, this getting old stuff is for the birds! Help me to grow old gracefully. I don't want to be cantankerous, cranky, or complaining during my latter years. Uphold me, comfort me, heal me, and give me strength when I feel weary and run down. I want to live to love my children, my children's children, and even my children's children's children!

Prayer Focus _____

Scripture Inspiration

_____

_____

_____

_____

Praying the Word

_____

_____

_____

_____

_____

_____

Prayer Prompt

_____

_____

_____

_____

_____

_____

_____

_____

_____

Day 19
Adult Children

☕ **Prayer Focus**—Words

📖 **Scripture Inspiration**

Death and life are in the power of the tongue, and those who love it will eat its fruits (Proverbs 18:21).

🕑 **Praying the Word**

Giver of life, enable my children to control their tongues so they will only speak words of life.

🌸 **Prayer Prompt**

Words are powerful. Guard my children's mouths. Help them to think before they speak. Do a deep, cleansing work within their hearts. May their words bring healing, encouragement, wisdom, love, grace, and truth to all those around them. Especially use their words to build up my grandchildren.

🍵 Prayer Focus _____

📖 Scripture Inspiration

_____
_____
_____
_____

🌀 Praying the Word

_____
_____
_____
_____
_____
_____

🌸 Prayer Prompt

_____
_____
_____
_____
_____
_____
_____
_____
_____

Day 19

Grandchildren

📖 Scripture Inspiration

Watch and pray that you may not enter into temptation. The spirit indeed is willing, but the flesh is weak (Matthew 26:41).

☉ Praying the Word

Lord, I pray on behalf of my grandchildren, asking that You would keep them from falling into temptation. Strengthen them to resist fleshly desires.

❁ Prayer Prompt

Jesus, You told us to pray to be delivered from temptation. I figure You wouldn't have commanded that if You didn't intend to answer that prayer. With You all things are possible, so please enable my grandchildren to resist temptation. Expose the lies of the enemy, and show my grandchildren Your light, that they might walk safely in it.

🍵 Prayer Focus _____

📖 Scripture Inspiration

_____
_____
_____
_____

🕑 Praying the Word

_____
_____
_____
_____
_____
_____

🌸 Prayer Prompt

_____
_____
_____
_____
_____
_____
_____
_____

Day 19
Grandchildren's Future

☕ **Prayer Focus**—Eternal Perspective

📖 Scripture Inspiration

No eye has seen, nor ear heard, nor the heart of man imagined, what God has prepared for those who love him (1 Corinthians 2:9).

☉ Praying the Word

Instill great anticipation in my grandchildren's hearts for their eternal future.

🌸 Prayer Prompt

Never let my grandchildren forget that this world is not their home. Fix their eyes on eternity. May every choice they make be decided with an eternal perspective. Place within them joy and excitement unspeakable as they look for Your return. Grant them eternal life with You in heaven.

Prayer Focus _____

Scripture Inspiration

_____

_____

_____

_____

Praying the Word

_____

_____

_____

_____

_____

_____

Prayer Prompt

_____

_____

_____

_____

_____

_____

_____

_____

_____

Day 19

Grandchildren's Character

☕ **Prayer Focus**—Giving

📖 **Scripture Inspiration**

Give, and it will be given to you. Good measure, pressed down, shaken together, running over, will be put into your lap. For with the measure you use it will be measured back to you (Luke 6:38).

🕙 **Praying the Word**

Giver of all things, work in my grandchildren's hearts until they are cheerful, extravagant givers.

❀ **Prayer Prompt**

Break through any fear or greediness, and teach them the joy of giving sacrificially, receiving abundantly, and then giving some more.

Children of the World

☕ **Prayer Focus**—Disease

📖 **Scripture Inspiration**

They brought him all the sick, those afflicted with various diseases . . . and he healed them (Matthew 4:24).

🕙 **Praying the Word**

Lord, heal Your children.

❀ **Prayer Prompt**

The multitude and scope of disease on this planet is overwhelming. But You are the creator of heaven and earth. Use missionaries, doctors, intercessory prayer, and miracles to save Your children from death and disease.

☕ Prayer Focus _____

📖 Scripture Inspiration

_____

_____

☉ Praying the Word

_____

_____

❀ Prayer Prompt

_____

_____

_____

☕ Prayer Focus _____

📖 Scripture Inspiration

_____

_____

☉ Praying the Word

_____

_____

❀ Prayer Prompt

_____

_____

_____

Day 20

Self

☕ **Prayer Focus**—Time with Grandchildren

📖 Scripture Inspiration

I have been reminded of your sincere faith, which first lived in your grandmother Lois and in your mother Eunice and, I am persuaded, now lives in you also (2 Timothy 1:5 NIV).

☉ Praying the Word

Lord, fill me with faith that overflows into my grandchildren's lives in such a way that my walk with You influences them for life.

❀ Prayer Prompt

Father, give me sweet, special days with each of my grandchildren. Allow me to deposit into the very fabric of their beings love, faith, and hope. Bind our hearts together through the building of memories and through moments that only the two of us share. Use me to impact their lives for Your eternal purposes.

🍵 Prayer Focus _____

📖 Scripture Inspiration

_____

_____

_____

_____

⊙ Praying the Word

_____

_____

_____

_____

_____

🌸 Prayer Prompt

_____

_____

_____

_____

_____

_____

_____

_____

_____

Day 20
Adult Children

☕ **Prayer Focus**—Rest

📖 **Scripture Inspiration**

Come to me, all who labor and are heavy laden, and I will give you rest (Matthew 11:28).

☉ **Praying the Word**

Dear Jesus, draw my children to Your side so they can lay down their exhaustion and anxieties and rest in You.

🌸 **Prayer Prompt**

Lord, I sometimes worry about my children and their busy, busy lives. Give them peace. Help them to trust in You for their future. Build their faith so that they look to You alone for help. Grant them sweet, sound sleep. Remind them to spend time relaxing as a family. Bless them with times of refreshment in Your presence.

Prayer Focus _____

Scripture Inspiration

_____
_____
_____
_____

Praying the Word

_____
_____
_____
_____
_____
_____

Prayer Prompt

_____
_____
_____
_____
_____
_____
_____
_____
_____

Day 20
Grandchildren

☕ **Prayer Focus**—Sexuality

📖Scripture Inspiration

Flee from sexual immorality. Every other sin a person commits is outside the body, but the sexually immoral person sins against his own body (1 Corinthians 6:18).

☉ Praying the Word

Lord, keep my grandchildren from all forms of sexual immorality. Teach them to run from temptation so that they may keep their bodies pure for Your purposes.

🌸Prayer Prompt

Almighty God, by Your great power and mercy, enable my grandchildren to keep themselves sexually pure all their lives. I pray that from this day forward they will save themselves for marriage and will remain faithful to their spouse for life. Establish a healthy sexual identity in them from an early age so they can enjoy this precious gift within Your wise and holy boundaries.

Prayer Focus _____

Scripture Inspiration

_____
_____
_____
_____

Praying the Word

_____
_____
_____
_____
_____
_____

Prayer Prompt

_____
_____
_____
_____
_____
_____
_____
_____

Day 20
Grandchildren's Future

☕ **Prayer Focus**—Care for Parents

📖 Scripture Inspiration

If a widow has children or grandchildren, let them first learn to show godliness to their own household and to make some return to their parents, for this is pleasing in the sight of God (1 Timothy 5:4).

☉ Praying the Word

God, may you be pleased to see my grandchildren taking care of their parents in their old age.

✿ Prayer Prompt

Put a deep love, respect, and appreciation in my grandchildren's hearts for their parents. Enable them to forgive their parents for whatever ways they may have let them down. Remind my grandchildren how much it pleases You (and ultimately blesses them) to honor their parents. Establish in them a holy sense of responsibility and a tender desire to care for their parents until the day their mother and father meet You in heaven.

Prayer Focus _____

Scripture Inspiration

_____
_____
_____
_____

Praying the Word

_____
_____
_____
_____
_____
_____

Prayer Prompt

_____
_____
_____
_____
_____
_____
_____
_____
_____

Day 20
Grandchildren's Character

☕ **Prayer Focus**—Mercy

📖 **Scripture Inspiration**
There will be no mercy for you if you have not been merciful to others. But if you have been merciful, then God's mercy toward you will win out over his judgment against you (James 2:13 NLT).

🕙 **Praying the Word**
Father, fill my grandchildren with Your mercy.

🌸 **Prayer Prompt**
Give them tender hearts toward others. Impress upon them the truth that only You know the whole story behind others' choices. Remind them not to judge, lest they be judged.

Children of the World

☕ **Prayer Focus**—Lonely

📖 **Scripture Inspiration**
I lie awake; I am like a lonely sparrow on the housetop (Psalm 102:7).

🕙 **Praying the Word**
Heavenly Father, comfort the children who feel all alone. Show them that You see them, because Your eye is on the lonely sparrow.

🌸 **Prayer Prompt**
Whether they are truly alone or have been rejected or hurt and feel that no one cares, wrap Your loving arms around them.

☕ Prayer Focus _____

📖 Scripture Inspiration

_____

_____

🕙 Praying the Word

_____

_____

🌸 Prayer Prompt

_____

_____

_____

☕ Prayer Focus _____

📖 Scripture Inspiration

_____

_____

🕙 Praying the Word

_____

_____

🌸 Prayer Prompt

_____

_____

_____

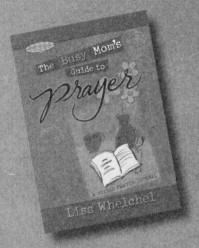
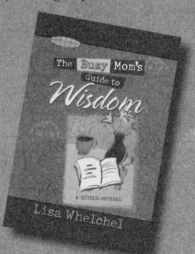